CON'...

Science and

Religion is a

Match Made in

Heaven

Jack Veffer

Toronto, 2014

ISBN: 9781497579859
ISBN-10: 1497579856

INTRODUCTION

This book is a work of fiction. It is, however, based on extensive research, intuition and imagination. Although much of its commentary is fictitious, it has its origin in the great scientific minds of history. I speculate that they might have offered up their enlightened observations in this way. While sometimes embellished, their commentary is largely factual and correct. The conclusions I have come to are based on scientific facts. I've given my imaginary characters names that sometimes belong to the real thinkers that I most admire. Some of the commentary comes from their actual words or writings and their actions are based on historical fact. But more often than not, their words and actions are what I imagined they might have said and done.

1

The book is divided into thirteen parts:

While writing this book, I arrived at the conviction that human beings are the only species with the capacity to contemplate their own existence and, as a consequence, that a different state beyond this present one exists.

As an individual searching for answers, that makes me unique, but at the same time common; for isn't everyone searching, on his or her own journey of discovery? The writing of this book also presented me with the opportunity to seek out and become more familiar with the mystery of what I have come to accept as a belief in a greater entity. Since we are all created beings, I hold out the hope that I will, someday, come face to face with my Creator.

In the book, I explore the harmony that must exist between spirituality and scientific discovery and maintain that there can be no contradiction between one and the other.

Further, I examine the preparation we must undertake to facilitate our destined encounter with God, since, no matter what our perspective on life, we share a common destiny.

I explore the nature of the individual identity called "Being" as well as the common identity called "Consciousness." I search for the interconnection between the two and why I think humanity has a common consciousness. My arguments are based on the fact that everything in the cosmos is made up of energy and that this energy has a purpose, a meaning, and an expression. Therefore, in the course of my research, I share what I've discovered about this purpose, and the meaning and expression in the vibrations of life we call sacred. We can observe this energy in the shape, color, and sound of things. We must be attuned to it. Energy manifests itself in such things as Leonardo Da Vinci's drawing of Vitruvian man, or the perfect proportions of Notre Dame Cathedral in Paris, or the exquisite shape of the Nautilus shell, a beautiful flower, the poetry of Rabindranath Tagore or the mathematics of Euclid. Unfortunately for some of us, these experiences often pass by unnoticed as we stumble through life, deprived of the signs that give meaning, beauty and purpose to our existence.

Everything in the universe, whether it is matter, energy or existence itself abides by two great sets of laws: thermodynamics and motion. In addition, there are rules that control the progress of the soul in this life as well as in the life hereafter. And the rules are not the same for this life as they are for the next. For the soul has both a purpose and a function, a "what" and a "how," if you like.

To facilitate discovery in my own imagination I have written in a child-like way to allow the child's gradual discovery of the miracles of birth and death and the realization that there is more to life than mere existence. I speak about a great mansion with many rooms, each with a particular name, and I roam through them, allowing the reader to tag along and glimpse the struggle for discovery from my birth to the present and beyond. As a student, I ask many questions, the answers to which come through the rhetoric of my learned teachers.

PART 1: MY MANSION CALLED REALITY—I THINK

Je pense, donc je suis.

—René Descartes, 1596–1650

Hello Jack, welcome to this existence called life!

What is this? Where am I? I rub my eyes. Nobody hears me. I'm cold and I was not cold before. All of a sudden I don't feel so good. "Ouch" Somebody hits me. It hurts. I hear loud noises. Somebody says "Breathe!" I start to cry and sputter and I have to take in air. What is that? It feels

5

good. I think I'll do it some more. Is that what breathing is?

I'm not happy; I think I'll cry some more. What's happening to me? Just before this, I was nice and snug and warm. I didn't have to do anything. It was perfect, but now I'm in this long narrow hall and it's cold and not at all perfect. I want to go back where I was before. I'm hungry. Where's something to eat? I'll cry, maybe that will help. Somebody picks me up. Ah yes, food. It tastes strange, but I think I like it. I open my eyes. Who are all those people? Before this I was alone. I liked being alone. Nobody came in. Now these people are all looking at me. They have silly expressions on their faces. Someone calls that a smile. They're laughing at me.

"Stop laughing at me!" But nobody hears me.

"He looks exactly like his uncle Bobby," someone says.

Uncle Bobby has a big nose. I don't like big noses. Mommy has a little nose. I want a little nose like Mommy. She smells sweet. I better look at Mommy because I want to look like her.

I think I'll cry some more. That seems to get their attention.

My tummy hurts. Now somebody is hitting me on my back. "Hey, stop that!" What was that sound? I feel better now. Someone calls it a burp. What's a burp?

Laughing and smiling is good I suppose. These people are all doing it. Maybe I'll try smiling. Boy I miss my snug, warm place. But I guess it's not too bad here. All I have to do is cry and somebody picks me up. I've got to remember that.

My Mommy is holding me in her arms.

"He's looking more and more like you dear" my Daddy says.

It feels so nice and warm in my Mommy's arms. I never want to leave. I look into my Mommy's eyes and I can see myself in her eyes.

"The eyes are like mirrors to the soul, sweet Jackie."

"What are mirrors, Mommy? Do I have a soul Mommy?"

A person can get used to this. It's not better than before, but different. I have legs and I can stand on them and walk around. Sometimes I fall over. Better get up. I think I'll do some scouting around. Let's see what's in the hall.

"Whoa, walk slowly Jackie or you'll fall and hurt yourself." Mommy and Daddy are smiling. Everything is good. Let me take a few more steps. Hey, there is a door. It's closed but I think I can open it.

A room called "learning"

Carefully I push against the door. The door opens wide. I step inside an enormous room. I know some of the people. There are Mommy and Daddy. "Hi Mommy and Daddy." I know the doctor and the nurse. I saw them when I was sick in the hospital room. I don't want to get sick again. They stuck needles into me and stuff. But who are all those other people?

"One plus one equals two. Two plus two equals four."
Who cares? Mommy and Daddy told me these are my
teachers and I have too study hard.

"Why do I have to learn Mommy?"

"Because otherwise you'll grow up dumb and you don't
want to be dumb do you Jackie?"

"When does learning end Mommy?"

"It never ends, dear. Hopefully you will never stop
learning. It's called knowledge, sweetheart."

A man dressed in a long black dress like a lady's is looking
down at me. He looks mad:" Do you believe in God?" he
says to me with a thundering voice.

"What is God, Mommy?" I ask, feeling rather important
because the man pointed at me when he asked the
question.

"You can't see God and you can't hear Him. But He's
around you, everywhere. Keep looking and one day you'll
find Him, Jackie."

I think I've had enough of this room called "Learning" for
a while. I'll see if I can find some fun rooms in my
mansion.

A room called "life"

I'm in the hall again. There is another door just a short way
from the room called "Life." The door is ajar, so I guess
it's OK for me to go inside.

"Dirty Jew" someone yells. Somebody yells and hits me with a stick.

"Stop hitting me. I'm not a Jew," I say, hoping they'll believe me.

Other people in black uniforms are dragging people away, men, women and children, and putting them in trains. My Mom and Dad are among them.

"Why are they doing this Dad?"

"Because we are Jews, Jackie. These are bad people, son. Don't ever forget what you saw in this room. From here on, you must hate all Germans. Remember when you asked Mom about God? Well here's your answer; do you think that if there truly was a God, He would let these bad things happen to us Jews?"

"Is there nothing good in life, Dad?" I yelled, as the train was leaving from the room.

"There are wondrous things in life. You must discover them," he answered, as his voice quickly fades away.

I open the door to get back into the hallway. I guess I opened the wrong door. This room; I don't recognize it. I'm worried I'm lost. There's my brother. "Hey Maurice, what is this room?"

Love and hate

"Maurice, what is hate?"

"This is the room called 'hate.'" Remember Daddy told you to hate and that is what you must do from now on."

9

"Maurice, what is hate?" A scared little boy, barely six years old, I ask this of my brother, who is four years older than I am and, I think, much wiser."

"You must hate all the Germans because they killed Mom and Dad. If you see one you must shoot him with a gun and if you don't have a gun you must beat him with a stick or beat him up with your fists. Above all you must never ever like Germans."

"But Maurice, I don't know any Germans. How can I hate them?"

"It doesn't matter if you know a German or not, you must hate anyways, because you never know if you'll ever meet one. So you better be ready to hate them all the time."

Wow, I want to get out of this room. Let me try this door. Wait, this room has a sign; I can barely read what it says. OK I see it now; it says "mistrust." Better go in here. I don't like the room called "Hate."

A room called "mistrust"

Mommy is squeezing me and she's smiling at me. I thought the bad Germans had taken her, but here she is.

I notice that I can do anything I want in my house. I can go back and forth in my house. Sometimes I notice many things I didn't see before. Sometimes there are too many things to see and everything gets all jumbled up and I can't really notice anything at all. This is all so confusing. There is so much to see and do. How can I learn anything?

"What are you doing Mommy?"

10

"I am hugging you, because I love you so much, dear." A wonderful feeling comes over me and the dark feeling that Maurice called hate is being chased away. Boy, I'm sure happy about that. I must get used to all these different feelings and sort them out, so I can avoid going into the "Hate Room" or any other room that gives me bad feelings.

In what looks like a large room with desks, an important looking man with a suit and tie stands in front of a blackboard and says: "Better remember that love is an antidote to hate."

"Mommy, what is love?" No time for an answer I guess.

A room called "change"

I don't like to hate. There sure is a lot I don't know. Mom is right I must never stop learning.

Somebody else is hugging me. I don't know this person. She has a nice face, but why is she hugging me? Only Mommy should be hugging me. The person says: "I love you Jackie. From now on I'll be your Mommy. I love you."

"That can't be! My Mommy and Daddy are coming back! I just saw them! They're the only ones that can hug me and love me! Not you!"

"That's not true Jackie. In your life you will encounter many people who will love you and some who will hate you. You must learn to accept that. Most importantly you must learn to love everybody."

It sure does not feel the same as when Mommy holds me and loves me, but it doesn't feel bad either. I can get used to other people hugging me and telling me they love me, I suppose. Can I trust them? No time for an answer I guess.

A room called "mind"

"Jackie, how old are you now?"

I thought, what a strange question. I don't know how to answer it with just a number, because so far my imagination has me jumping through my various ages, sometimes going forward and other times backwards in time.

"Who are you and why do you ask this question?" I asked, intrigued.

"I am your enquiring mind replete with a healthy dose of curiosity and the reason for the question is simple. We've all been born into this life with one simple mission and that is to learn. So far, you've skipped through your short life learning things by accident. You've skipped from one experience to another with no input from you. It's called intuitive learning. Learning that way is important, of course, but at a certain age we must all learn more formal knowledge."

"Learn what?"

"As best we can, we must learn about the mystery of life itself. What it is? Why are we here? The three Rs."

"What are the three Rs?"

"They are reading, writing and arithmetic. These are the foundation for your formal education and without them you will be severely handicapped as you navigate through life. This type of learning will require assistance from learned teachers. So what I will do, from hereon in, is to introduce you to the best, most erudite teachers who will help you to gain this knowledge."

"OK that sounds fair."

"The first one of your teachers I will introduce you to is Dr. Deepak. With the help of many others, he will help you understand the mysteries of life and teach you what you need to know."

"Hi Jackie. Let me introduce myself. I am Dr. Deepak."

Where is my mind?

"Dr. Deepak, where is my mind? Is it in my head?"

"Let me preface my answer by telling you about my background. I am a medical doctor trained in the healing arts, using the conventional tools of Western medicine. As such I employ different methods to heal, including drug therapy. To be sure, it is a trial and error method because no two people are the same and often react differently to the drugs we might prescribe. But because there is no shortage of synthetic drugs, we find that if one does not work we can prescribe another, until we get the desired result: to treat the symptoms of your disease, fervently hoping that we also get rid of the underlying cause of your disease.

But I also have a degree in Eastern medicine, in Ayurveda. This is about the science of life, a system for the prevention of disease and promoting longevity. It is the oldest and most holistic medical system available today and it is thousands of years old. I also established a foundation to promote what I term 'mind/body spiritual healing.' I claim, for a fact, that your body can heal itself through your mind.

"Today's thinking about health is to concentrate on how to live better with disease. So, if we can control the pain and mitigate the effects of the disease, people believe that it is the only thing that can be done; so there has been a shift away from education to preventing disease, and to the inevitability of eventually succumbing to disease. As a consequence, we devise ways to incorporate disease into life, instead of educating people to live healthier lives and preventing disease. That is the sad state of affairs in Western medicine today.

"Now that you know some of my qualifications, I will endeavour to answer your question by asking you one first: Jack, do you think that your mind is part of your brain?"

I reply, "Doctor, I think the question is rather redundant. Of course it is, the brain is where all the thinking goes on."

"Well you might think so, but you're wrong. My experience as a doctor in multiple disciplines allows me to view the mind from different vantage points. We know, for a certainty, that the mind and body share the sum total of all knowledge. So it is evident, therefore, that all your cells are also the recipients of all the same knowledge and experiences that your mind possesses. They can and do continually communicate with each other. Your body is comprised of approximately 100 trillion cells. The knowledge is imprinted in every single cell of your being. The ability of your mind lies in its capacity to function as a standalone, complete unit and is the mirror image and storage unit for everything your brain processed in the past, the present and the future. The mind retains that information forever. It is like the disk drive of a computer. Your brain communicates with all the parts in your body and vice-versa, and is inherent of who you are and how you function and can be likened to the "central processing unit (CPU) of the computer. To be sure it also stores a myriad of information, but it is information required to keep functioning while you are in this life and in this body.

"So Jack, write this down; better yet, commit it to memory, because it is important:

> *[The Mind is] an embodied and relational process that regulates the flow of energy and information, consciousness included. Mind is shared between people. It isn't something you own; we are profoundly interconnected. We need to make maps of we because we is what me is.* [1]

I'm overwhelmed and say, "Hold on now. I don't really care about what you're telling me and I don't get it. But since we're at it, you might as well explain it to me. What does it all this mean? What on earth is an 'embodied and relational process'?"

"I sympathize, Jack. Please don't get angry and frustrated. That won't get you anywhere. Just trust that what I and my colleagues will tell you will make some sense; perhaps not right away, but eventually. Until then, try not to jump to conclusions too quickly about the relevance of these and other topics that we will explore. I've asked myself many of these same questions. So let me share with you some of

---

[1] Daniel J. Siegel, 1999, *The Developing Mind*, p. 3.

what one of my colleagues, Dr. David Drum has to say about the universal mind: "William James used the term 'transcendental mind' a continuum of cosmic consciousness that exists in a higher dimension and subsumes individual minds. The Catholic theologian, Pierre Teilhard de Chardin, posited the existence of a membrane of consciousness encircling the globe, that would be enhanced anytime the consciousness of any one individual in the world is raised. Leonard Shlain writing in *Art and Physics* goes further and describes the universal mind as an *overarching, disembodied universal consciousness that organizes the power generated by every person's thoughts.*[2]

"And Shakespeare said it well, when he had Macbeth lament while he was praying '*My words fly up, my thoughts remain below. Words without thoughts never to heaven go.*' We may be part of a much larger entity existing in the space-time continuum with an agenda we are not aware of. If the individual self-reflective mind knows that it knows, universal mind knows everything, everywhere and anytime. The Talmud expresses the subtle relationship between individual reflective mind and universal consciousness in the dialogue between Abraham and God, where God begins by reminding Abraham, '*If it weren't for Me, you wouldn't exist.*' Abraham thoughtfully replies, '*Yes, Lord, and for that I am very appreciative and grateful. However, if it weren't for me, You wouldn't be known.*'

"So, Jack, here is some more insight to complicate the issue: the big question we need to ask is: Why is there something rather than nothing? In his book *A Universe from Nothing* physicist Lawrence Krauss states, 'Nature comes up with surprises that far exceed those that the human imagination can generate.' He reminds us that our galaxy is one of 400 billion in the observable universe, and that star stuff and earth stuff are largely the same; that every atom in our body was once inside a star that exploded, a supernova. So our bodies are literally made of stardust. And all the structures we can see, like stars and galaxies were created by quantum fluctuations from nothing. Another enigma is that empty space has enough energy to dominate the expansion of the universe. Frank Close, professor of physics at Oxford in his book *Nothing* reminds us that an atom is a perfect void, 99.9999999999999 percent empty space. Its emptiness is profound. But it is filled with powerful electrical fields. A finite region of empty space having all matter removed will still be filled with energy and this energy fluctuates spontaneously, turning into electrons and positrons lasting only for 10 to the -21 seconds and fluctuating into and out of their virtual existence within one thousandth part of an atomic radius. Modern physics suggests the universe could have emerged out of the vacuum. But Close concludes his book with the thought, 'I am confronted with the enigma of what encoded the quantum possibility into the Void.'"

I am confused and ask, "what does he mean when he says he is confronted with the enigma of what encoded the quantum possibility into the Void?"

Dr. Deepak tries to relieve my confusion, saying, "We can only conjecture. We know that what is termed empty space in the universe or 'Void', as Dr. Krause refers to it, is far from being empty. It is energy that is simply not discernable to us in its present state. Because we can't see it, does not imply that it is not there, just as you spent your entire narrative on the subject of the existence of the soul

17

without really knowing that the soul exists. Only if you assume or believe in the possibility of its existence can you explore the possibilities of its existence. In that way, we can conceive that the universe—and possibly anything else outside of the universe—may in fact seethe with energy identifiable as virtual particles and antiparticles that erupt spontaneously into being. These are contained in dimensions that we are unaware of presently. These new discoveries may provide answers to some of cosmology's most fundamental questions: what lies outside the universe, and, if there was once nothing, how did the universe begin? Then, of course, we can always fall back on the Higgs boson, the building block of the universe, the so-called 'God Particle.' The boson itself provides the necessary proof for the existence of the Higgs energy field. We can liken the Higgs field and the boson particle to electricity and the light of a lamp. We don't know what electricity is but we see its evidence in the light it creates. If you see the light then you know that electricity exists. So for the boson particle to be there, you know that the space for that particle is there too. So it is with the belief in God, that to know the existence of God, we observe God's qualities and attributes in His Prophets. Since the Higgs particle was observed at the CERN lab in March of 2012, we're pretty sure that the Higgs energy field exists."

"I think I understand. Belief in something is such a great asset. Without belief we could not start to explore the possibilities."

"That's right, Jack, and we should thank David Drum for his profound insight. But we got off track a bit, so let's get back to your question about what 'embodied' means. Everything we experience, every memory or emotion or thought is part of a process, not a place in the brain! That is what is meant by 'embodied,' as in 'contained' or 'part of.' Relational means that it is related to something. So it means that we are all part of the process and we're all connected. So the process is being able to do something or use energy in other words. There's nothing that is not energy; even mass is energy. Remember E=MC squared? Hence, the mind is an embodied and relational process (action) that regulates the flow of energy and information. I know it's a pretty abstruse subject, but you'll eventually get it."

A greater entity: God

"Jack, can you believe in a greater entity, something that is greater than you or me?"

"Do you mean: can I experience the presence of a greater entity?"

"Well no, not in the physical sense, but in a purely spiritual sense. You will encounter people in your life who will profoundly affect you by their goodness, their wisdom and their empathy for others and by their ability to make you see good things that you previously could not see. You will be granted a glimpse of that greater entity by gazing into the lives of those appointed-by-God-individuals, those stainless mirrors, who reflect the perfection of God. These are people like Jesus the Christ and Moses, Mohammed and many more. Let me introduce you to one of them."

"Wait a minute. Hold on. I don't believe in God. My father told me that God does not exist and that anyone who believes in God is a weakling. I don't know who these people are, so why should I pay attention to anything they might tell me. Who is this individual anyway, who you want to introduce me to?"

"Oh, so you *are* paying attention. I thought that I'd lost you there for a minute. Let me tell you this about God. It may help you to think of God not as an entity, a person or someone you know as a person, like Jesus, but rather like a destination, because our ultimate goal is that we want to attain His presence, be there in that special space we call heaven. Let's face it, we can't know who God is; we can only know what He represents, that beautiful place we've heard and read about. So try to open your mind and let it soar; let your imagination run free so that it conjures up an image of the most beauteous, serene space you can imagine. We're told it's a thousand time more beautiful than that. So why do I say that God is not an entity?"

"I don't really know, but I'm sure you will tell me."

"You're right of course. God, we are told, is unknowable. We don't deal well with unknowables. We therefore call Him God and we made Him male and identified Him as Jesus the Christ. And then we even give Him a recognizable face. We know intuitively, that this is wrong, because, if everything in the universe is energy, then God is the pristine, purest energy. Don't confuse this with everyday energy, because God's energy is perfect, as represented by the qualities and virtues we all try to attain throughout our lifetime on earth, qualities such as love and empathy and many others, of course. All of God's qualities are important for the growth and maturation of our soul. We all want to be like God, or rather, what God represents.

"Let me give you an example: we all agree, I think, that the ultimate challenge of skill and daring on earth is mountain climbing and the epitome of that skill is to climb Mt. Everest. If you climbed Mt. Everest without really knowing what it represented it would be just another mountain. But because of its name, its notoriety, its reputation, based on the many attempts and failures, it represents the ultimate, the model for courage and the greatest challenge mountain climbers will ever attempt. Reaching its summit is to have attained the perfection of their skill, a true testimony. So if it is courage we need to get to heaven, all mountain climbers who climbed Mt. Everest would get there, right? But it's not that easy, because God's place represents the destination we will attain after our mission here is complete. It requires a lot more than courage. It takes will, perseverance and an unshakable faith, along with the qualities we talked about before, qualities such as love and empathy to attain God's presence.

"So don't be so hard on yourself. You can do this. All you need is a healthy sense of humour, to laugh and try to enjoy yourself. Remember that I am your imagination and you'd better pay attention to what I am thinking, because I am you. I am the object and the subject, like a book and its title.

"Before we go elsewhere in your mansion let us go directly to your "brain room" to explore the wonders of that most sophisticated organ inside your mansion: your brain. Always enter without knocking, because without unfettered access to your brain room, you will definitely be incapable of going anywhere else. In other words no matter where else you reside in your mansion, you will always be in your brain room, too."

Love, compassion, equanimity and humility

"Hi Jack, this is Deepak again. As one of your mentors, I must tell you something that you must always remember: the acquisition of knowledge is of paramount importance for the soul's progression into the next world of existence. To be sure, that is not all that's required, because the acquisition of knowledge is merely one step in a two-part process. The second step is the application of that knowledge for the common good."

"Dr. Deepak, how do I know that what I do is helping to improve the human lot?"

"That is a very good, but complex question, which has occupied the minds and actions of thinkers throughout the ages. If you ask yourself the following question and answer it with a simple 'yes,' then you're on the right path. The question is this: Is what I do or what I am about to do of benefit to people?

"Then you must gain an understanding of morality and ethical behaviour. These are only two of the many other factors that will affect your actions. You must learn them all. Do you understand what I'm saying?"

"Well, sort of, but not really."

"That's not really an answer. Let me explain. In acquiring knowledge that may be beneficial to others, you must keep in mind the aspects of love, compassion and an attitude of humility in any action you undertake. Next you need to determine whether your actions will somehow be of benefit. But you must be careful, as there are actions disguised as altruistic which could be purely selfish or immoral or even perverse. For example: if you help someone with the idea that he will repay you somehow later, for example with money or an even bigger favour, then that help is not really helping him, is it?

"We must also explore what the soul requires for its passage into the next world. It's the soul that signals when its time has come. So, in other words, we need to know what qualities need to be added to the energy.

"We need to add love, a special kind of love that includes the close ties you have with others, such as your parents. This love is binding. It is usually the type of possessive love that makes you feel cuddly, warm and safe and makes you feel that you belong. It is a nurturing love with a strong social component. It makes you feel that you are an important part of the human family. When you cultivate that love, it includes the qualities of not only love, but also compassion, equanimity and humility."

"I don't get it," I said. "Energy is energy, isn't it? The soul's energy does not change, does it? And by the way, I don't think we can know when we are about to die and I think that's probably a good thing."

"Yes, the soul's energy does change. It must change, for the soul is ready to move to the next stage when it has obtained what it requires for that journey. It depends on it. Let me explain it in a way that might help you grasp the importance of this conformity. Let's assume that your soul is a piece of a puzzle with billions of pieces. The name of the puzzle is 'God's world.' The difference between this and an ordinary puzzle is that the pieces in God's puzzle are not yet shaped to fit into the 'God's world' puzzle. Your piece will be shaped by the way you live your life.

Each piece, by the way, represents an individual soul. At the end of your life here, if you've lived your life correctly, your puzzle piece will have attained the exact size and shape to fit in God's world puzzle. If it is not the right shape, it won't fit properly and you'll barely be able to discern what God's world represents. The God's world puzzle will never be complete. It just keeps on growing and growing so long as there are new souls born. So now do you see the importance of learning and applying what you have learned?"

"Yes I do, Deepak. Thanks. Maybe you can answer another question that troubles me: what if my piece of the puzzle, to use your analogy, is not the right shape to fit into God's puzzle. What won't I be able to do?"

"I can answer you by giving you the example of water, or H2O. In this physical realm, water can switch form from cold or solid ice, to warm boiling water, its boiling point, to steam. Although these states are worlds apart, they are all still the same chemical substance called H2O. It can manifest itself in different energy levels. So if, for example, you want to drink a glass of H2O you must change its energy. It has to do with purpose and function. If your purpose is to quench your thirst, then the water you are about to drink must be in a liquid state. The proper relationship between the two is crucial. Same with your piece of the puzzle, or your soul, which must be in the perfect condition to properly see God's world and function in that world."

The purpose and function of the soul

"What," I ask, "is the purpose and function of the soul?"

Deepak replies: "These are synonymous aren't they? But they are different in this instance because *purpose*, here, means *mission* and *function*, in this case, means *service*. So, the fulfillment of our mission on earth is the applied use of our God-given talents.

I ask, "Does that mean that we must gain spiritual eyes so that we can see Him?"

"Well," said Deepak, "it certainly means that we must not only learn the attributes of God, but we must also use them for the good of humanity. I'm sure you are beginning to realize that this is about the seventeenth time I've said that to you! It's that important! In this context, we can actually understand the meaning of the life and education of the soul, since we only have this one lifetime to work on perfecting our soul. Therefore, we have no time to waste! If we live our life without having fulfilled our mission, it will have consequences in the next life. By the way, everything that comes into existence has a purpose. Our purpose in this life is to know God. Our mission in life is to serve God."

"But what if I don't believe in God? What happens to my soul then?"

"To answer that question, you must realize that, to the best of your ability, your words can describe a vast range of things. Sometimes not very well, I may add. But we try the best we can to use language to communicate complex ideas that often defy mere words. Sometimes we use words to attempt to describe events, social phenomena, or people and entities. Using the word 'God' for example, an imaginary entity, is one such word. It does not describe a human being, but rather an entity that is beyond our comprehension and defies any other description. As you well know, there are other such words that are used to describe the same entity, such as 'The Primal Point,' 'The Creator,' 'The Light,' 'The Primal Source,' 'Point of Adoration,' 'Yahweh,' etc. It seems that we have done that to facilitate a more common understanding of the word 'God.' He has become popularized in history, in re-occurring Biblical events and in His perfection. His essence may not be knowable to anyone, but His attributes are mirrored perfectly by the privileged few He has appointed as His mouthpiece. That is how we perceive Him, not as a knowable essence, but as a metaphysical truth most of us embrace because we need to take guidance from a more perfect life for the perfecting of our soul.

Deepak went on: "The goal is to eventually attain God's presence, and we know that the only way to do this, is to gain spiritual eyes with which to see Him."

"What happens to the soul if it doesn't gain that knowledge?"

"It seems evident from what we've gleaned so far, that the soul does not stay attached to the body after the completion of its time on earth. It takes its leave and goes somewhere, to an undetermined space, one that seems neither familiar nor comforting and does not appear to be the soul's ultimate destiny. So where, you might ask, is that space? We can only surmise that if that space is not God's presence it must be some way-station."

PART 2: MORE YOU NEED TO KNOW

TO GET TO HEAVEN

The room called "reality"

Deepak now says, "Jack, what I will tell you now is basic to understanding reality: first, you must understand that the physical world is not reality; rather, it is your perception of things that is your reality. In metaphysics, physical reality can only be perceived as a mirror image by the non-physical mind."

I am confused and ask, "Deepak, can you please explain what a non-physical mind is? And are we really the centre of the universe?"

27

"That's an excellent question! If you believe in God, it is easier to accept the presence of a non-physical mind. Atheists would have a real problem in accepting the existence of a non-physical mind. They only rely on empirical evidence for their reality. The definition of the non-physical mind is that thinking is done with the brain, but the reality is that the non-physical mind does not physically depend on the brain for its perception. It is for this reason that even though an image is formed in the brain, the non-physical does not discern it. The non-physical mind receives a mirror image, a reflection if you will, of what the brain perceives through the five senses, and it is the reflection of that image, in the mind, that becomes our reality. As a matter of fact, the mind is not part of the brain; it exists, even though it seems that it is an integral part of the body, outside of the brain."

"So are you saying that the mind is not a part of the brain?"

"Yes, that's what I just said. The brain is the center of your thoughts and your brain is comparable to what they call, in computer jargon, the CPU, the central processing unit, able to process thoughts, make complex calculations, process and arrive at conclusions, make decisions and then determine the course of action. But, of course, we all know that the brain does not necessarily make the best decisions! So the brain is, indeed, an integral part of the mind. But so is the rest of your being. Your body, your organs, every cell in your body is a part of your mind. Your unique identity is in every cell that makes up who you are. All the parts working together are the sum total that makes up your non-physical mind. So the dichotomy is that we are, at the same time, three different entities; we are the observer, the observed as well as the observation."

"Deepak, if what you say is true, that we are the observer, the observed and the observation, can we therefore surmise that we are the center of the universe?"

"No, you cannot. There is only one centre of the universe and that is God. All you can take away from this now, is that we, as souls, are near the centre and as one of many billions of cognizant, rational bits of energy, we have the responsibility and the unique opportunity to make it our own by perfecting this energy. If all goes right, that energy will join with God. By the way, the fact that you are able to ask this question, hear the answer and draw conclusions is proof that you are conscious, that you exist. It seems reasonable to conclude that the mind is not physically dependent on the brain for its awareness. It gives a restated meaning to the state we call consciousness. The mind does not do the thinking. We know for a fact that it's the brain. However, the conclusions are drawn and actions taken in close consultation with the mind, with the result that a mirror image is permanently stored in the mind. It can be accessed again and again from that point on, for it will never be lost. Of course, the most important evidence of the non-physical mind is that when the soul separates from the body at death, all the knowledge that was accumulated over a lifetime on earth stays with the rational soul.

"Now I suppose that you are going to ask me whether this can be proven without having to die first. The simple answer to that question is no. There is some science that has shown that people who suffered a near-death experience were able to see things while they felt they were disengaged from their bodies. When they "re-joined" their body, these people were able to tell of their near-death experiences. For now that must suffice. You should

29

cultivate a certain amount of acceptance, with a healthy amount of inquisitiveness, of course. Since few answers or proofs are available right now, it will allow you to accept on faith alone things that cannot be proven."

Our spiritual nature: Prayer and meditation

"Deepak, I do believe that I have a better understanding now of why we must pray and meditate and why we should make these actions a part of our daily routine.

If it is true—and I have every reason to believe that these truths will become more self-evident—then prayer and meditation are the means for educating the rational soul and therewith become more mature humane beings. Am I correct to say that prayer and meditation are not the only roadmap for the soul? However, I somehow think that it is an important ingredient in the recipe, and that since the soul is energy, its maturation and its journey into the afterlife require this spiritual food for its progression. I find it helpful to explain this period of preparation, by thinking about the baby in the mother's womb. The baby in the womb must develop all the qualities for existence in this life: limbs for walking, eyes for seeing, ears to hear, and a nose to smell. Of course, it has no real need for limbs, eyes and ears when living inside its mother in its watery reality, nourished through the umbilical cord. But then, suddenly, there is no more room in the womb. Birth "kills" the foetus! Yet we know that birth is not fatal, and so switching from foetus to body presages the passage of death from body to soul. Does that make sense to you?"

"That's good, Jack. I think you've got it."

"So," I continue, "in addition to our physical development, we seem to need help to tell us how we can attain the spiritual qualities that enable our souls to progress. This guidance comes from God through His emissaries. It demonstrates that we're not alone and that we all share a common purpose.

"So does it make sense that when we're released from our bodies, what we've learned becomes important for our souls to attain God's presence? Without God's guidance, through prayer and meditation, will we have difficulty in attaining God's presence in the next life?"

Deepak looks at me seriously and replies, "That's exactly right."

Near-death experiences

"Deepak, what do you know about near-death experiences?"

"Jack, there are many accounts from people who suffered cardiac arrest and during their 'death' come back to life and report having had a consciousness far beyond the what they experienced in their previous life. And their accounts all seem to have common elements.

For example, the out-of-body sense that they were watching themselves on the operating table and watching people fuss over them. Then of going down a long, white corridor, of meeting loved ones along the way, and of assuring them that everything was all right.

"So you must ask yourself: how is that possible? How is it that when the heart stops and no or low brain activity is observed can consciousness continue in an altered state? All I can say is that we have the testimony of many people attesting to the same facts. Let me introduce you to one of these people, a doctor, a neurosurgeon, in fact, whose name is Eben Alexander. He can tell you his own story!" Dr. Alexander greets me warmly and shares his experience:

"Hi, Jack! I must tell you first that before my near-death experience, I was skeptical, as a scientist and a doctor about NDEs. And although I was sympathetic when my patients reported having gone through one, I always attributed their experience to low-level brain function and the brain secreting a particular protein that would trigger such visions. That is, until I myself fell into a coma during a bout with e-coli meningitis. I must preface my comments by saying that e-coli meningitis is very rare in adults, particularly when there do not seem to be any discernable external causes to explain the disease. In my case, there were none. My brain simply crashed. The disease attacks the neo-cortex, the outside of the brain. For seven days I experienced the most incredible sights and sounds I have ever seen or heard, while my neo-cortex was completely non-functioning. As you probably know, the cortex is responsible for memory, language, emotion, visual and auditory awareness and logic. My near-death experience was so wonderful, that I cannot describe it in mere words. I did attempt to describe my experiences down in my book called *Proof of Heaven*. Jack, I urge you to read it! Let me read some passages from it so that you might get a taste of what I went through:

> *My experience showed me that the death of the body and the brain are not the end of consciousness that human experience continues beyond the grave. More important, it continues under the gaze of God who loves and cares about*

each one of us and about where the universe itself and all the things within are ultimately going. The place I went to was real. Real in a way that makes the life we're living here dreamlike by comparison . . . a visible darkness, like being submerged in mud, yet also being able to see through it . . . Consciousness, but consciousness without memory or identity—like a dream where you know what's going on around you, but have no real idea of who or what, you are . . . How long did I reside in this world? I have no idea.

Then I heard a new sound: a living sound, just like the richest most complex piece of music you've ever heard . . . .I began to move up . . . and in a flash I went through an opening and found myself in a completely new world . . . a beautiful, incredible dream world . . .Except it wasn't a dream. Though I didn't know where I was or even what I was, I was absolutely sure of one thing: this place I'd found myself in was completely real . . . Brilliant, vibrant ecstatic . . . I felt like I was being born . . .Not re-born again. Just born . . . Below me was the countryside, green, lush . . .It was earth-like. . .Imagine being a kid and going to the movies on a summer day. Maybe the movie was good or not. But when the show ended, and you filed out of the theater. . And as the air and the sunlight hit you, you wondered why you wasted this gorgeous day in the theater. Multiply that feeling a thousand times and you still won't be close to what I felt like where I was . . .[3]

"That's a fascinating story, Dr. Alexander."

"Jack, fascinating or not, there are people who don't accept these accounts and who are attempting to find a

---

[3] Alexander, *Proof of Heaven*, pp. 9, 29 and 39.

plausible, scientific explanation for the near-death experience. They sometimes call them trivial and not worthy of investigation. I'll introduce you to one. This is Dr. Wendy Wright, a neurologist from Emory University. She has some alternate views on NDEs."

"Hello, Dr. Alexander. I've long been an admirer of your work. In my research as a neuroscientist, I maintain that near-death experiences are merely a result of endorphins in the brain. When these chemicals are released, any one or all types of phenomena can occur: a person might see a light, or walk down a long corridor and experience a deep sense of peace. They might also sense that loved ones surround them. These visions are little more than tricks the brain plays on us."

"You may say that, Dr. Wright. Prior to my own near-death experience, I had the same opinion and dismissed these phenomena with the same determination as you. As a neurosurgeon, I maintained that they were merely naturally occurring phenomena that deserved only scant attention. Of course, I was always sympathetic with the people that told me such stories, but I didn't believe them, until I had the experience myself. It was so real that I can no longer dismiss them as just some type of low-level residual energy left in the brain. It is more than that; it is the energy emanating from a special place that seemed reserved for me. I have no name for it but I now know it is there, waiting for us all when we pass from this earthly life. I don't know what that energy is or where it is located, but what I do know is that it is uniquely mine. And to prepare for this, we need to ask what the qualities are that the soul needs to acquire in order to progress from its state at the time of death to progress to this exalted space.

"I would say that these necessary qualities include love and the belief in an entity greater than ourselves. This recognition and loving attitude translate into actions that affect others in a positive way, such as kindness, love, empathy, generosity, hope and equanimity. I am sure you can think of many others if you set your mind to it."

"Thank you for that, Dr. Alexander. But please tell me: how can the soul's energy meet in the afterlife with God?"

"Jack, I don't have an answer to that question right now, but we know from the laws of thermodynamics that energy is never lost and therefore the soul's energy, ready or not, moves to another plane of existence after death. I don't know that I did anything special to prepare my soul to wind up where I did. All I know is that the space was somehow reserved for me when I needed it. As you know by now, energy changes from one state to another to become usable again in its new state. Energy has a number of different forms, all of which measure the ability of an object or system to do work on another object or system. In other words, there are *different ways* that an object or a system can possess energy. I now feel that, just as with all forms of energy, such as electricity, sound or motion, so it is with the soul's energy. In this earthly life, it is merely observing, learning, becoming "charged," in order to fulfill its purpose and obtain a roadmap for its destination, its ultimate mission in another state. This energy is infused with God's knowledge, whether we know it or not. Qualitative evidence for this is demonstrated in our attitude, love, empathy…, towards our fellow man. The soul is then born, perfect, in its new existence. Without these attributes I think the soul would have difficulty in encountering the presence of God."

35

Deepak re-joins us here, saying, "Thanks Dr. Alexander. I have a few thoughts that may shed some further light on this very difficult subject. It seems to me that it is the understanding of language and its many varied meanings that gives us clues about the way to attain God's presence. But does that guarantee that we can get there?"

"Just a minute, you two," I say, jumping in. "I don't mean to be disrespectful but can either one of you tell me why you use different words to indicate what appears to be the same location. You seem to be interchanging 'Heaven' and 'God' and 'God's presence' all at the same time and for the same idea. Do they all mean the exact same place? And the other question I have is; if your soul cannot reach this location, where does it wind up?"

"Those are great questions, Jack," Dr. Alexander replies. "Let me try to answer the first part and I hope Dr. Deepak will concur: yes, Heaven, God and God's presence and so on, all do point to the same place. The reason for that is simple: the conventions of language and what we've come to accept as common understanding using words and body language. Some habits are easy and trivial, such as "yes, OK, and all right, which all mean more or less the same thing, right? But other conventions are more difficult to grasp, such as the language about the soul. We don't talk about that in our everyday language and so we need further clarification. I'm glad you brought it up. Keep asking questions.

"Now let me address your second question. I can only relate it to my own near-death experience. I think that Heaven must be separated by degrees, and based on my own experience; I could call one of these places within Heaven 'Nearer to God' and the other 'further from God.'

These degrees of separation are based on my own observation: the 'further from God' part is like a visible darkness, like being submerged in mud. But I was also able to see through it . . . I had consciousness, but it was without memory or identity, like a dream where you know what's going on around you, but you have no real idea of who or what, you are. For example, I had no idea how long I had been living in this world. But then, as I drew nearer to God, I heard a new sound, a living sound, like the most exquisite, most complex piece of music I had ever heard. I began to move up and in a flash I went through an opening and found myself in a completely new world, a beautiful, incredible dream-like world. Except that it wasn't a dream. Even though I didn't know where I was or even what I was, I was absolutely sure of one thing: this place I'd found myself in was completely real, brilliant, vibrant, ecstatic. I felt as if I was being born. Not re-born again. Just born. I think that my time in the mud was further from God. A way station where I had to remain, for whatever reason I do not understand. After the required time there, I was born. I don't know whether I ever reached the stage that I would call 'closest to God' or 'being at one with God,' but whatever or wherever my soul winds up, I now know for certain that my place in Heaven is reserved. What is yet to be determined, based on how I live my life here, is what degree of closeness to God in Heaven I will occupy."

The psychology of communication

I accepted Dr. Alexander's explanation and then turned to Deepak and asked, "Now what were you saying about language and understanding the meaning of language."

Deepak took up this theme again, saying, "Jack, let me ask you, whether in your mansion you have a room called 'language'? Somehow I don't think so. I suggest you get yourself a room for language. Language is not always effective to convey complex ideas. There is more to the literal understanding of words to execute these ideas. Ideas are rarely literal. It's more a feeling or thought and how do you communicate those? How do you communicate or interpret ideas about God, heaven and hell, good and evil and so on… Mechanically doing what you need to do without really understanding the idea won't always get you where you want to go. And yet people who are incapable of speech, but who in their attitude to others show forth the qualities of love and empathy will be able, without ever uttering a word, to be close to God in their next life."

Now I am impelled to ask Deepak a metaphysical question: "Does one's belief in God vary one's perception of reality after death?"

"I noticed you have no God room either Jack. You do unprovable thing. Of course, if you're skeptical about what I have told you, go on the Internet and type in NDE or near-death experiences and it will bring up quite a number of verifiable cases of people that have gone through one and described it. The stories they tell of what they experienced are not only fascinating, but eerily similar. Most important in our conception of reality is the recognition that perception *is* our reality. You perceive it; therefore it is real. This axiom works just as well for the condition we call the near-death-experience. It is in fact so real, that it is the very definition of what we talked about earlier, that your perception is your reality. Yet we try to explain away this experience by saying that it did not happen, or that it is a chemical reaction, that is results from a residual part of your memory acting up, or a complete memory-dump, like the computer does when it 'senses' an imminent computer hardware failure."

"I get it. You can see the reality of yourself outside of your body. Do you mean that while in your body you remain constrained to an earthly existence we can call normal, but outside of your body anything is possible? Is that about the size of it?"

"I guess so. You restrict your earthly life but your non-physical abilities are virtually unlimited. So it is possible that you can influence what you can be in life by training yourself to be the best that you can be. In theory you can be anything that you wish to be. Of course, it is the education of your soul that is the primary objective while you are in this earthly realm. It has always been about knowledge and using that knowledge to help yourself and others. That's the legacy that binds us together as an evolving humanity. Your capacity is what determines how and what you become. Of course, you are a product of where you came from; your parents, teachers and your own unrestrained effort enable you to achieve what you want. The flip side of that argument is also true. Not only can your abilities be severely held back by your parents and your teachers, but you can be restrained by your own doubts about your ability to see what you can do. We're all influenced by one another and affected by the actions of others."

The concept of non-locality

Suddenly, Deepak asks me another unrelated but interesting question. "Did I ever talk to you about a concept that is now fairly well known in quantum physics called non-locality?" I'm stumped for a moment.

"Well," he continues, "the greatest minds in history—in particular Einstein—did not accept the concept of non-locality. His view differed from that of his contemporary, Rabindranath Tagore, the Indian writer and poet. I'll tell you about their famous meeting at Caltech in 1930. First though, let me explain what non-locality is."

"Deepak, you've already confused me enough by what you've told me so far. Why talk about yet another concept I've never heard about, and have trouble understanding?"

"Jack, Don't be afraid of words. Non-locality is important in understanding your consciousness and your being. It's important for you to grasp the fact that everything is related to everything else in the cosmos.

"Non-locality or non-local reality is one of those great mysteries in quantum mechanics that has a great impact on our existence. Even though it has confounded some of the greatest minds, it has nevertheless been mathematically proven to exist.

"It goes like this: Every particle has a twin, even if these particles are separated by millions of light years. Here's a simple analogy: if I tell a particle here a funny story, then its twin, that is located elsewhere a million light years away will laugh at my funny story. Not only does the funny story transcend distances but it also does so instantaneously, as if there were no separation between these particles. Einstein, during his now-famous meetings with Tagore at Caltech in 1930, called it spooky science and maintained that it violated the rules of cause and effect. First, he said it went counter to Newton's Laws of motion, particularly Newton's third law: For every action there is an opposite and equal reaction. It also defied Einstein's rule, which held that nothing could travel faster than the speed of light. So no matter how fast the interaction was, the interaction between the particles could never be instantaneous. Tagore claimed that it did neither, since the interaction between the twin particles transcend the time-space principle and was therefore not bound by the rules of causality or the speed of light restriction.

"We now know that Einstein was proven wrong and that Tagore was right, since John Bell's non-locality theorem proved that the theory of instantaneous interaction between two identical particles was correct, no matter how far apart they were from each other."

"But Deepak," I question, "Before we go any further, I have two important questions: first, why on earth should I care about non-locality? And second, why didn't Einstein get it right away?"

"Well, Jack. The answer to your first question is that there exists a harmony between all science and religion. It is important that you understand and appreciate the interconnectedness between particles.

41

The fact is that everyone's existence is conjoined with that of every other being, and this means that at one time or another; we've shared most of all our particles with everything else in the cosmos. The particles that make up your unique being have been continually shared by everything else in the cosmos. Some scientists say that our body and its parts are renewed approximately every year; that is, you grow a new spine, blood vessels, heart, lungs, skin, etc. annually! Thus, we're not so different one from another. The genes we think are unique to us are not so unique after all, as we share 58% of the same genes with a banana and some 98% of our genes with monkeys! Of course, what does make us different from everything else is our human ability to think rationally, that is, to reason.

So, based on all the knowledge we've gathered thus far, it is not so difficult to speculate that there is a life hereafter; a life that is unconstrained by time and space. Another aspect to consider is what we call 'intuition.' As I just said, we know, for example, that each particle in the universe has at one time or another been shared with everything and everyone else. Therefore, it is perfectly reasonable to believe that these particles continue to communicate with each other. We could call these interactions intuitive, empathic, sympathetic, random or accidental. But, more often than not, these communications are not random, simply because the terms of reference we use—such as intuition, accident, design and random are not well enough understood to provide a contextual understanding of these terms. Some thinkers have a much broader understanding of intuition; for example, Mona Lisa Shultz, in her book *Awakening Intuition* looks upon intuition not so much as a 'gift' bestowed on some of us, but rather as yet another undiscovered dimension with finite rules. Remember that I stated that there are 57 dimensions, of which we know and vaguely understand the meaning of only four. It may well be that, just as intuition may be viewed as its own dimension, so, in a broader context, other conditions such as accidental, or design, random and chaos may also be seen as dimensions, each with their own, as yet, undefined rules. Who knows, right?

I listen quietly, trying to understand, while Deepak continues: "The confounding thing about life comes when you view it from two different vantage points: quantum physics, the theory of the infinitesimally small—and the world of Einstein—the theory of the very large. We see that many of the principles from both disciplines and the conclusions we draw from them seem to be at odds with one another. That is, of course, not possible. A good scientist will readily admit that what can be proven in one discipline cannot be disputed by the other discipline. So we need to find the common ground between them."

Here, I cannot resist jumping in with another question: "Deepak, can you define what the body is? I know that it is made up of a number of common elements. So is it a 'thing' or not?"

Deepak reflects for a moment and then says: "Jack, remember this: The body is not a structure; it's a process."

PART 3: WHAT YOU MIGHT ALSO

WANT TO KNOW

The brain room

There is hardly any room to move around here. It is full of some kind of spongy material.

"What is this room?" I ask.

"It's your brain room," a voice answers. "The control room of all your thoughts and emotions. Whether you have an urge, an itch or an injury, everything comes here first to be analyzed and to decide on an appropriate reaction. How you deal with some things after the analysis

45

is, of course, mostly your free choice. For example, if you are a celiac and you deliberately eat bread, your stomach sends a message to your brain that you don't feel well. The natural response would be to no longer eat bread, since you know that it will make you feel bad. So, why do you decide to keep on eating bread? Do you see what I mean by free choice?

"By the way," the voice continues, "there are many functions in your brain room that don't require your active involvement. These have been automated and thinking about them before taking action would be redundant. Without these automated responses, your brain could not sustain life. For example, these are inquiries from your vital organs, such as "Hey, up there, how about some oxygen for the lungs here, so we can breathe!" or the beating of your heart, so that it can pump the blood throughout your body. You certainly don't need to think about such things."

To my surprise, the voice turns out to be none other than psychiatrist Sigmund Freud! I am most curious to ask him what we take with us from this existence when we die. Freud replies, "the short answer to your question is that we take everything with us from this life, because the experiences of life are all considered knowledge. As you know, all knowledge is stored in the universal subconscious. The long answer is somewhat more complicated and for that, you need to know more about how the brain functions. As I understand it, the soul separates the useful information that is essential in our next existence from that which is non-essential or of no use in that realm."

The brain room revisited: Things you wanted to know about the brain but didn't know to ask

Dr. Freud says, "Jack, let me introduce you first to a famous neurologist, Dr. Richard Petty. He will give you a fairly thorough introduction to the brain and its function."

"Good morning Jack. My name is Richard Petty. Please feel free to take notes because I am going to talk to you about how 100 billion nerve cells communicate with each other.

"The human brain weighs around three pounds and is not particularly beautiful, unless you like the look of a cauliflower. It is the most highly developed organ in your body, the most powerful and versatile tool you possess, a miracle of design and sophistication. Let me give you a quick tour. The cerebellum and the brain stem assist you in your movements and aid survival functions such as breathing. The cerebrum is the largest and most developed part of the brain; it lets you be creative, feel and think; it stores and retrieves memories; it is what gives you personality and is in charge of the body's conscious state and conscious movement.

"The brain never stops learning and, when exercised regularly, has the ability to actually remap itself. This is especially significant after a stroke or a brain injury. The learning process itself has four phases: memory, attention, processing and sequencing."

I interrupt to ask him about the significance of the left and right hemispheres of the brain. "I hear that there has to be a certain relationship between the hemispheres in the brain in order for us to be in a well-adjusted state. What can you tell me about that Doctor?"

"You're right, Jack. There exists a harmony between the left side and the right side of the brain and the two must be in sync to operate efficiently. It is like the harmony between logic and spirituality or the two wings of a bird.

"One side is no less important than the other, and each is crucially important. For, as you already know, preparation for the life hereafter is dependent on our gathering knowledge in this life. To be sure, the left side enables us to interact with others in this life as social beings, allowing us to understand order, social structures, conventions and communication, while the right side allows us to appreciate artistry and the beauty in all things.

"I hope this has been helpful and that you can now resume your conversation with Dr. Freud. I know you are anxious to learn more about the soul."

Stumbling around in my soul room

"Dr. Freud, I don't get it. Can you explain to me what it means to get into heaven?"

He seems stumped by my question and says, "I am afraid I'm the wrong person to answer that. Remember that I was the one who confused many generations by claiming that humans are not only libido-driven creatures, but that the sex drive was their sole driving impulse. Hardly worth a ticket into heaven or even close to a way station to heaven, wouldn't you say?"

"Yes, I've heard that before, but what did you mean by "libido-driven?"

"The libido is the sex drive. So, to put it into the vernacular, it means that all we want out of life is to have sex and that we'll do whatever is necessary to get it. That is what I believe truly defines us. So, I really think you need to put this question about heaven to someone else, someone who believes that people have the capacity to be something else besides driven by their sexual impulses."

Body, spirit and mind

"Jack, Deepak here again. I'm sorry that Dr. Freud wasn't able to help with your questions. So let me continue. Since I've done considerable work in trying to understand the human psyche, I think it would be helpful to you if I list the three aspects that I think make us who we are. There are three sides to the human dimension: the first is purely physical, that is, the body; the second is the purely spiritual; and the third is the rational mind.

"Let's first consider the body, made up of many moving parts which require regular attention through exercise and proper diet for health and rest for recuperation. Over time, like all moving parts, these wear out as you know and it is vitally important that you understand and take good care of your body, for it is the temple of your soul and you are its custodian. Without the body, your soul cannot develop properly. Some people think that the development of the body is what matters most in this life and become fanatical about it, with the result that it becomes the sole purpose in their lives, at the expense of the development of the mind and the spirit.

49

The spirit is that essence which allows us to see life with the eyes of the heart.

The rational mind is what assists us in the education of our soul, by applying reasoned thought to everything we do and learn. Reason is the unique capacity that no other animal except human beings possesses."

"Dr. Deepak, would it be fair to say that everything emanating from the rational mind has to do with "sequential knowledge?"

"It is true that the knowledge of this world of existence stays in this world and is not portable to the next. Harmony with the material world is very important to us but knowledge of the material world is not spiritual in nature and is of limited use in the next world. Solely concentrating on material knowledge is a distraction that will impede spiritual growth. Many would have us believe that what we learn and what we enjoy for our bodily gratification is of lasting importance and the opposite is actually true. If we emphasize the ephemeral comforts of this life at the expense of spiritual progress, it will not help us.

And it is also true that in the next world, sequential time does not exist, that is, no past and no future. The essence of what we recognize here as past, present and future becomes one indefinable entity of time."

"Dr. Deepak, can you tell me what heredity is and how it affects the outcome of our lives?"

Here, Deepak pauses for a moment and then explains; "heredity is the pattern of intricate biological traits or characteristics that are passed on from parents to their offspring through the genes. These patterns are permanent, although they are sometimes interrupted, obliterated or damaged. Nevertheless, once they are established, they are transmitted into your mind as clusters of knowledge that remain forever embedded as part of your consciousness."

"Can you please tell me then. How much do we know about the human brain, its capacity, its powers and limits?"

"We know very little, actually. Let me put it in simple terms so that we can measure, quantitatively, the limits of your knowledge. Let's say that the number 100 represents the total capacity of the brain. A hundred years ago, our collective knowledge would have been about one out of a hundred. Today we know perhaps three out of a hundred. It is still a relatively small number, but a quantum leap in comparison with the past."

The answer does not satisfy me completely so I ask the question that has occupied man for thousands of years "Was man created by God or not?"

"I can only answer that question in an oblique manner; it does not really matter whether or not you believe in a God or nature or the universe. What you actually believe will ultimately fall under the general heading of "faith." Although some would argue with the word "created," there is no denying that we are somehow "created" since we obviously did not create ourselves. Therefore, no matter what we think it is, there is a force "out there," even if we came about from chaos or by accident, which started the ball rolling. Of necessity we must subscribe to the idea that we are the created, for before our creation we did not exist. And the Creator, however conceived, is a

51

force that operates outside our sphere of knowledge, whether or not we have religious convictions. If you have the notion that we came about by accident, without any help from an outside force, from the primordial ooze, then you should also be able to envision that something much less complicated than the human frame, let's say a car, could also come about in the same way. After all, a car is a million times simpler than any human being. How likely is it that from a lump of iron ore, and using the same premise that the human being came about from nothing with no intervention or prior design, a car could suddenly emerge? How long would we have to wait before the car appeared? A thousand years? Or a million or a billion years? So, you see, Jack, if you think that's a ridiculous comparison, then the emergence of a human body, without any assistance, by sheer accident, is even more ridiculous, because we are exponentially more complicated than a car."

PART 4: ENTER THE GREAT ROOM

Enter the room called the "divine dimension"

"Jack, you may now enter the greatest room of your mansion," says Dr. Deepak, gesturing with a grand wave and smiling before the impressive entrance. "This is the room which stores the secrets of your mind."

"Doctor, what is this Divine Dimension you're talking about? How did you come upon this farfetched idea of yet another dimension—as if we're not having trouble enough trying to keep track of the dimensions we already have!"

"It's quite simple, really. I figure that the special kind of knowledge that we need to progress into an everlasting

53

existence, once it is gathered, needs to be stored somewhere for safe keeping and retrieval."

"I suppose, you're right there."

Dr. Deepak continues, saying, "So the mind and the soul, after originating from a special space, occupies its own dimension. This is the space I call the Divine Dimension. It is at the centre of your mansion, in this great room. It is a reservoir for all of your spiritual experiences. It is not a part of the brain room. It is important that you realize that learning is never completed, you must never stop learning; you'll find knowledge everywhere. Even though undiscovered knowledge already resides within your Divine Dimension room, you cannot use it in your next life or in this life, for that matter; that is, unless you've discovered that knowledge first. It is also true that you know more than you think. You already have a great deal of knowledge that you don't have to think about anymore. It's called subconscious knowledge. It's also in your room and forms a part of your total knowledge base.

"But," he continues, "this leaves us with the conundrum whether to store all things not understood in a separate room we might call the intuition room and to use that knowledge without comprehending it, much as we use electricity, without really understanding what it is. Or is it better to merely cast them into your rejection room for lack of evidence of their existence? The answer to the question is obvious: Use them and trust that you will eventually find an answer."

This kind of patient faith I find hard to accept and I say, "Some of my teachers would have me believe that, since I can't perceive or explain something by means of logic or through one or more of my five senses, I should reject it. There are just too many things that remain unexplained so I feel that I must accept these unexplainable things in good faith for now."

"Jack," continues Dr. Deepak, "in life you will have to make choices in a dichotomy of ambiguities, a conglomeration of different, incompatible feelings, where the profane and the sacred, the unethical and the ethical, the sinful and the virtuous all coexist and the choices you make between them will continually confound you. It therefore becomes a primary objective to endorse the explainable and to accept the unexplainable and attempt to reconcile, in your own mind, the reason for both. It does require sustained investigation, but it's a worthwhile exercise. Find the balance of acceptance between tangible and intangible knowledge, between that which is based on science and that, which is based on faith, and learn to accept both equally. Stop narrowing your understanding of life through book learning alone. Instead, look for knowledge wherever it resides."

"Now that sounds like sound advise, Doctor," I reply, relieved that we're finally getting somewhere.

"By the way, the following is also true: the realization that we hold ourselves back from achieving greatness. Many think it necessary that we must live our lives within the narrow pronouncements of who we are told we are, safe from the possibility of failure and, as a consequence, never quite achieving our true potential for the fear of trying? Do you think that if you limit your reach for excellence, you will protect yourself from failure? The answer to that question of course is no and that once you understand the nature of the Divine Dimension you will realize that failure has no place. The Divine Dimension is where you will discover both ethical answers and answers that shape your destiny. They shed more light on the mysteries of birth and life, death and immortality."

The Divine Dimension, besides allowing you a glimpse into your own mind, is also the repository for the sum total of the human experience and a resource for the spiritual maturation of humanity and the eternal soul."

"Doctor Deepak, please explain more about the existence of this divine dimension."

"I'm not sure, Jack, that the explanation I'm about to give you will satisfy your question. We're all engaged in this reality, some more than others and we attempt to feel the pulse of the rhythm of life. We've arrived at this point in humanity's evolution through trial and error. All of humanity's experiences have been inscribed, as a permanent record, on the virtual blackboard of life, for all to explore and we're all the most recent result of the triumphs and tragedies of a bloodstained human history. You must learn from it. You can help in making it better. If you listen, it will provide you with answers to all your questions about creation, existence and the reason for existence. Moreover, thanks to Albert Einstein, you know that since energy is matter and vice versa ($E=MC2$) you will realize that knowledge is energy and needs to be contained and that I have chosen to name this compartment the Divine Dimension. Knowledge, being of form as well as substance, is embedded in that part of your being called the mind. So the mind can be likened to the finest instrument ever devised. It is able to play back in perfect replication all of humanity's experiences; the exquisite as well as the profane. The only receptacle that is worthy to hold such as fine an instrument as the mind is the Divine Dimension.

"I believe that most of us aspire to live a meaningful life, a purposeful life that will make a difference, a life filled with hope and expectation, and above all a life that embraces love, the most potent of all emotions. A meaningful life can therefore be characterized as one that encompasses a rhythm of excellence. Rhythm is the measure to gauge the cadence of your accomplishments, while excellence is the measure to check whether you've attained a standard of performance that encompasses that rhythm. You never quite achieve excellence but you keep striving for it. Sustainability in the pursuit of that excellence is the key to true success. And finally, the purpose in this life is to leave your indelible mark on the book of life. We should all strive to leave a legacy of good deeds and virtuous behaviour. This then becomes the model for moral and seemly conduct for those you leave behind."

"Doctor, before now I had never heard of this dimension. It sounds like an interesting viewpoint, but one that I have some difficulty in accepting. I am still trying to figure out the time-space dimension. Let me ask you this important question that has troubled me for some time: "Is it permissible to accept a proposition for which there is no evidence; for example, the existence of a Greater Entity?"

"Jack, if you're asking me whether there is a God, I don't know the answer to that. No one does, but I think the best answer I can give has not so much to do with whether belief in a Supreme Entity is vital in the scheme of things, but whether that belief animates you to be the best you can possibly be and at the same time to do good things for others beside yourself."

Still troubled, I reply, "Dr. Deepak, from my vantage point, with the knowledge that I have, and having been a witness to the miracle of life, I would say that it cannot have come about through an accident of nature. There exists an underlying order that points to a predestined occurrence, a metaphysical point in time where a Creator must have said 'BE' and therefore we 'ARE.' To think of chaos as having brought all this about and acting upon our human destiny, is a fallacy."

"You might be right at that Jack."

Containing knowledge

"I have still another question to ask: you mention a container that you call the Divine Dimension which holds your individual knowledge and the Universal Knowledge as well as your soul and your mind. All these are all pure energy. How can it be contained in a receptacle?"

Dr. Deepak answers me thoughtfully. "Do you remember Albert Einstein's claim that Energy is also Matter? We talked about this before. Whether it is matter or energy, it needs to be contained. Knowledge needs a container because it is information that has been captured, thought about and has to be stored somewhere for future use. If you had nowhere to store it, how could you retrieve it? Things like the knowledge of breathing or your heart beating, or your brain processing thoughts. This is all contained knowledge, long ago resolved to be put to use as the exigencies for being alive. We now do these things automatically, without having to further think about them. These occur simultaneously and automatically, but if they hadn't been stored somewhere, your subconscious that performs these functions would have no access to that knowledge. You would not be able to take a breath because you would not be able to retrieve the knowledge of breathing and your life would come to an abrupt end for lack of air in your lungs! The same goes for thinking and the beating of your heart; these are learned behaviours, stored in your subconscious. So, in a manner of speaking, both energy and matter need what you might call a "bucket." To make it easier, you can think of your buckets as having different colours: the blue one holds your Universal Subconscious, the universal knowledge that we all share for the necessities of life like breathing; the red one holds your Personal Knowledge that makes you uniquely who you are; your soul is contained in the white one; the yellow one holds your mind.

So you see that your Divine Dimension is made up of this rainbow of colours with so many different hues that you cannot possibly count them all. At the end of your earthly life, your Divine Dimension, replete with all the knowledge from your buckets and your soul, joins all the other Divine Dimensions with all their own buckets to fulfill your common destiny with the Oneness.

Once you tap into the Divine Dimension, you will recognize it as a world where, when you listen well, the answers to questions about the experiences of your life become relevant.

Jack, you can immerse yourself in your Divine Dimension which, as you may recall, is located in your great room; you can gain access to it from each of the rooms we have already visited and those we have yet to visit: the Prayer and Meditation Room, the Divine Proportion Room, the Divine Gateway Room, and the Observation Room. Passage into the Divine Dimension will allow you to explore your Universal Subconscious, train your mind with new knowledge and educate your eternal soul. The application of this knowledge for the greater good will give your life more meaning and purpose. You can never have too much knowledge, for it is the basis upon which you can make your earthly existence better, stronger and more meaningful.

"Of course, you will have important questions about your inter-connectedness with others, like your father and mother, siblings and yes, even strangers. So you need to look outside the safety of your mansion to learn about current affairs, globalization, an understanding of the world. You need to know about the relevance of institutions in society, about a healthy diet and exercise, and so many other things. If you don't look outside your own mansion, you will be missing out on one of the greatest opportunities to learn about your own life and that of others.

PART 5: WHERE THERE IS HOPE

THERE IS LIFE

The room called "hope"

"Mr. Veffer will you please give us your definition of hope?" Louis Van der Braecken, my teacher in ethics, wakes me from my reverie. Startled, I begin to mumble my response: "Uhhh... My definition of hope is, like, you have a feeling that something good will happen, I think sir."

"OK, apart from the stunted grammar, I'll accept that explanation. And tell me, Mr. Veffer, are we the only animals capable of this feeling of hope, or are other animals capable of experiencing this feeling too?"

"I do believe, sir, that, consciously or unconsciously, all living things experience hope. For example, if an oak tree, at the end of the growing season, sheds its fruit and loses its leaves in the fall, it is with the implicit hope that a new season will start the growing process, like a period of renewal, all over again. The question is whether the tree consciously knows it or whether it expects it because hope is built into its genetic memory. It may well include a sense of wellness, because an unhealthy tree loses its capacity to thrive as it was meant to do. That raises the question of destiny or preordination. The tree is also affected by the cycles of life. These are cycles of birth or renewal and cycles of maturity and eventual destruction. It determines the end of the cycle for that particular oak tree but not its species."

"Hold on now, Mr. Veffer. These are complex issues and deserve much more thought and discussion, at a later date perhaps. Your thoughts on hope are somewhat rudimentary, but I think you're on the right track."

"Thank you sir, but I do think that hope is tied to faith. Faith is an attitude that we possess which we cannot really explain rationally. Faith that God exists is just such a feeling and cannot be proven beyond a reasonable doubt; and since it cannot be proven, we accept it with feelings of hope and anticipation for better things to come. Because of a universal consciousness that has been cultivated over the eons of time, we have conceptualized an ideal life that is in store for us, and because of that, if our life is not ideal, a better life always remains a possibility. Without an image of what life should be, we could not entertain hope.

Finally, even without hope that life here on earth will improve, we have hope that in a future existence things will be better."

"Now wait a minute. Do you mean to say that if you do not accept the existence of God you cannot have hope?" I wonder if he is trying to bait me or if he is asking a legitimate question. Better tread softly and see where we go from here. So I continue: "Hope is what I would term a 'standalone' capacity, not really requiring other sentiments, I believe. It is not dependent on faith and the belief in God. It is part of everyday language that implies that better things will come after bad times, just as day follows night."

PART 6: ALL YOU WANTED TO KNOW ABOUT THERMODYNAMICS

About the earthly life of the soul

"Hello Jack, this is Carl Jung speaking. Everything in the universe or universes is made up of energy. So it is reasonable to also envisage God as pure energy. But of course it is unthinkable to conceive of Him as mere energy. To think of Him that way seems somehow sacrilegious. It is also inconceivable to think of God as having mere human qualities. Ask yourself: how do we know what they are and how do we recognize them? God, in His infinite wisdom, appoints certain outstanding individuals and gives them these very qualities. We have come to know them as Prophets or Messengers of God; Jesus the Christ, Moses, Mohammad, are but some of these. They are the stainless mirrors that show the rest of us the perfect reflection of God's qualities. These 'Messengers' have been appointed for our benefit. They are special, superhuman, sacred beings from whom we can gather the knowledge to educate our souls. So it is that we are born with souls that are a blank slate on which in this earthly existence we must develop the God-like qualities that are manifested by God's messengers, such qualities as love, empathy, truthfulness, honesty, mercy, and so on. After the soul is so elevated by these qualities, it will ultimately be released to the universal energy source and, equipped with these godlike qualities, it can then attain God's presence.

"Language is such a poor way to communicate, isn't? Our bodily frames, automobiles, trees in the forests, houses, your favourite food, in short all things, everything that you observe as solid matter is ultimately but vibrating atoms, in other words, energy. So, too, is your eternal soul pure energy; and so, too, are all forms of sentiment.

"Energy is discernible in vibrating wave patterns and any event that occurs or any action we undertake within the energy matrix leaves its own pattern or footprint. Luckily for us, energy is slowed down enough in this life so that it is observable and we can actually experience the consequences of our actions. Everything we do as individuals, such as walking, sleeping, thinking about the hockey game, hoping that Canada will win an Olympic gold medal, in short everything we do interacts with other activities within the energy grid and has consequences for all that are involved in the billions of activities that occur concurrently at all times. Many clash with each other. We do all interact with energy, sometimes in ways that are detrimental to us and to universal harmony. It is during those periods that we grow better or worse physically, mentally or spiritually. There is a confluence of occurrences that affect us in positive and negative ways.

"We speak of the fourth dimension as the space/time continuum, but I think it should be the space/time/energy continuum. We can interact in positive ways within the dimension, causing good positive things to happen or conversely we can interact in a negative or malevolent way, thereby eliciting dark energy (dark, as in 'not good') to emerge. The choice is always ours. The distinct vibrations caused by our interaction with energy or the interruption of the universal energy flow—resulting in the various experiences of life—aid in fashioning our destiny in the hereafter. These interactions can cause us to be in disharmony within the energy continuum and thus, ultimately we need to be reconnected to it. These disconnected occurrences establish distinct life patterns that make us all unique and different. We use what we've learned to interact within the energy grid in a way that sometimes helps us and at other times is not so good for us. Thus, we must optimize our connectedness to the entire energy spectrum, without really interrupting it. Sometimes these interruptions disconnect us and send us on tangents that can manifest themselves in disease or ill health and a general disconnect in our lives.

"One basic lesson you can take away from what I've told you is that everything is composed of energy. Don't ever forget that. Your harmony with this oneness of energy is your state of well being. Do I sound a little like a Buddhist monk? Notwithstanding the 'God-like' connotations of my statement, it is a profound truth that we should be able to test and prove to ourselves that it is better to live in harmony than in disorder."

A little nonplused by Yung's surprising statements, I say, "this is all very interesting, but I would like to make an observation of my own: I have this nagging feeling that us possessing a soul is merely something that someone concocted to make our earthly life seem more interesting and more meaningful. And now, since many embrace this idea, it has become part of the language of life. It has become a popular notion that each of us possesses a unique, eternal soul that continues to exist beyond our earthly demise. So let me ask you this question doctor: what proof is there that this is so?"

"Good question, Veffer. It demonstrates that you're thinking and that you're not ready to accept anything at face value. To better address your question let me introduce you to someone you might not know, but who will be able to make things a little clearer for you. His name is Nicholas Léonard Sadi Carnot. He was born in 1796 in Paris, France. The reason I'm introducing him to you is because Sadi Carnot is recognized as being one of the first to link all energy with the laws of thermodynamics, which in turn govern energy. Even though he made one of the greatest scientific contributions to explain the properties of energy he died at the tragically young age of 36 and thus could not complete this important work."

"Hello Sadi, why are your ideas on energy and thermodynamics of interest to me?"

"Open your mind, young Jack. As you have learned by now, everything in the universe is made up of energy and

everything in the universe conforms to the laws that work upon this energy. These laws, as stated by Einstein and others, are known as the laws of thermodynamics; that is, the study of energy transfer from one state to another, or from one state of producing energy to a state of equilibrium, where energy can no longer be transferred. I know that may seem like a fuzzy explanation, so let me bring Einstein back into this conversation. As you know, he was the one who related most of the theory of light— ergo energy—to the laws of the universe, specifically, that light has mass and bends, thereby also conforming to the law of gravity. He'll be able to explain much better than me how these laws of thermodynamics explain the existence of your soul and your soul's capacity in an everlasting existence."

Thermodynamics

"Hello there, Jack. Do you remember me? $E=mc^2$, the theory of relativity and all that? I will try to describe for you how these laws of thermodynamics affect your soul by using my theories, OK?

"Let me begin by saying that all the energy in the universe conforms to the same laws of thermodynamics and because your soul is pure energy, therefore, so does your soul. Does that make sense to you?"

"Yes, I think it does, so far"

"Good. We'll concentrate on the first and the second laws of thermodynamics to explain the soul's phenomenon: the first law of thermodynamics says that energy is constant and can change from one state to another, but that energy can neither be created nor destroyed. Hence, if it is true

that the soul exists and the soul is composed of pure energy, it exists forever and it can never be destroyed. After death, it continues to exist in a changed state, laden with all the experiences from its bodily life, but it remains the energy that is your soul with its unique characteristics. Do you understand?" He pauses while I give thought to this statement, he then continues.

"The second law applies to entropy. Very simply, energy—like heat for example—always flows from hot to cold and never from cold to hot. There comes a point in this energy flow when all the energy is of the same temperature, when there is no more energy flow and the energy has reached equilibrium; in other words, no more heat is produced when it reaches this state. That is the law of entropy: the energy still exists, but it has changed its state from usable to unusable."

"Dr. Einstein, this is all very interesting," I interject, "but how does it prove the existence of the soul?"

"Well, Mr. Veffer, it seems to me that you have no problems in understanding sensory information, such as hearing, smelling, seeing, feeling and tasting, but that you cannot seem to grasp ideas that you cannot experience with your five senses. Expand your mind, Jack. Your body is a bundle of energy. There's a lot going on at any one time. Your heart is beating, blood is flowing, your stomach is churning and your lungs are taking in air. It's all energy. The mystery, of course, lies in knowing the catalyst for this continuous flow of energy and in what happens to the spent energy? Let's explore the energy spectrum. Let me first reiterate that energy and matter are really one and the same and that one of the fundamental aspects about consciousness and the concept of our reality, yours and

mine, is that consciousness is energy and that consciousness itself must therefore conform to the same rules of gravitational pull as all other matter or energy. It is simply that gravity cannot be merely regarded as some kind of 'emergent phenomenon,' secondary to other physical effects, but that it is a 'fundamental component' of our physical reality. In other words it bends."

Conflicting theories

"We are all conflicted by one theory that says that a God created our existence 'in His own image' and by an opposing theory that states that the universe came about by accident. Both tell a fascinating story. The first tells of the story of creation and a 'First Force' that created existence. The second talks about a theory of chaos. However, that is not a point I want to explore here. It doesn't matter whether or not you believe in an energy source that started existence—in what has been called the 'big bang,' or this Primal Force, which then split this tremendous energy source into four separate forces: gravity, electromagnetic energy, the weak nuclear force and the strong nuclear force. Science and religion come together in explaining that on this point there is consensus in understanding the significance that everything sprang from a primal force. In religion, we call it God and in science we call it the unified field or string theory. Scientists have also come to agree on a handful of principles that have fused a theory of exquisite simplicity, called the 'standard model.'

"The standard model suggests that there exist only two classes of indivisible particles, called quarks and leptons. As it turns out, the right combination of quarks and leptons can make up any atom and therefore any type of matter in the universe. It is also significant that all matter is held together by any one of the four known forces I outlined earlier. It sounds pretty simple doesn't it? But hold on to your hat. Did I say indivisible particles? Scientists have long theorized that there are still smaller particles than quarks and leptons. We now know, as Deepak pointed out, that by smashing these particles together they split. That is how we discovered the Higgs boson and dubbed it the 'God particle.' We can only wonder if even that is truly the smallest or if we will perhaps discover something smaller yet!

"We also know from experience that gravity is something that holds us to this earth and if it were not present we would fall off the earth. But what gravity actually consists of is less well understood. All that I can say is this: the laws of attraction and repulsion do not apply in the universe the same way as they apply to our everyday existence; in other words, to you and me. In the universe, attraction and repulsion work simultaneously. Structures are formed and destroyed at the same time. If you liken the universe to a bowl of thick soup, you can visualize everything in this thick soup, vegetables, pieces of meat, and everything else, floating together seemingly independent of each other; yet we can observe an underlying order; in other words, everything is connected: you and I, trees, planets, and so on. Of course, to make things more realistic, the other dimension that we need to be aware of, is that the soup, as it is in the universe, is not contained in a bowl. Another compelling enigma is that in the universe, planets collide, stars explode and everything seems to be freely floating. There is no explanation for these phenomena. They just are."

I am skeptical. "Wait a minute. Something doesn't jive. You said before that everything is energy and that therefore all energy must comply with the laws of thermodynamics. For that reason I think that it is not likely that these laws do not apply to the planets and the universe alike."

"You're right of course," Einstein replies quickly. "Except that when the big bang occurred, everything that was previously one single point of enormous energy was split into component parts that, temporarily at least, showed forth an expanding view with different characteristics of the same thing. Now we're trying to find the unified theory that can explain everything. Ironic, no? It lets us observe things in a solid state, when the expanded energy fused with others and became solid matter, while others remained pure energy. It's incredible that science is now looking at a vastly expanding universe and trying to find the meaning of its origin. And the irony is that one of the forces, electromagnetic energy, governs the very thing that has no mass, the photon, one of the building blocks of the atom. And the universe, as we know it, is made up of empty space or to use another word 'nothing' and then there is something. Is it because the space is reserved? And yet all the component parts of the big bang seem to conform to the laws of attraction and repulsion.

"So," he continued, "the question still remains, why is it that things in the universe defy these laws of attraction and repulsion. Why do they push and pull at the same time? Is it that we perhaps don't know enough yet? Why do the stars not abide by the laws of thermodynamics? We know that the electromagnetic force works with, and is, energy and the rules for this energy are pretty much defined in the laws that govern energy, that is, the laws of thermodynamics. We also know that everything is energy even though its state can be observed and made to behave as matter, such as light. Whatever its state, however, it affects us and interacts with our life at every moment of our existence. Just as this first event, the big bang, sprang from a primal point, the point of unimaginable density; it not only split the energy force into four, but it also spewed matter into a continually expanding universe. Therefore, we conjecture that at one time, before the big bang, this was all condensed into one. To be both participant in and observer of this event is a testament to the importance of our role in this life. Ironically we are also the observation. Without our testimony, this event could not be witnessed and therefore did not 'happen.' Our consciousness is the only reality to anything that happens in the cosmos.

Consciousness is reality

Einstein continues. "Let me give you an example of how I came upon the idea that our testimony to events is reality. Let's suppose that you and someone you know do something together, for example, discover a cure for cancer. You both did it together and you're both well satisfied that you did the job well. But let's say that your partner, who was part of the process of invention and witnessed it, develops Alzheimer's disease and does not remember the event; in his mind, it never happened, but you witnessed and participated and you know for a fact that it did take place. Who is right and who is not? Now suppose that both of you have Alzheimer's and neither of you remembers what you did together. You did not write it down and the cure remains unrecorded. Was the cure discovered? And so it goes with everything. If we all develop Alzheimer's and we no longer recall all the events that formulated man's evolving maturation, then none of it took place, right? It simply never happened. Do you see what I am saying? That is why the role we play in this conscious state with all its knowledge-seeking and sharing is vital not only to our ever-evolving soul but to all created existence.

"The next part of the puzzle is that the soul has a clear responsibility to fulfill its mission to gather knowledge, so that it will be able to progress to another level of existence when it leaves the body. How and when is the soul 'ready' to leave the body?"

Mission complete

He has left me breathless and I ask, "What do you mean by that? When the body dies, the soul must leave the body. I don't understand the question."

"Well," Einstein explains, "the idea of the soul's ability to leave the body with its mission complete—as opposed to having to leave when its mission is incomplete—must make a difference to the soul. The fact that the soul is not 'mature' can be likened to a baby growing inside the mother's womb and having to be born without having grown its legs, for example. That will make it very difficult for the baby to get around unaided. So the baby in the womb has to fulfill its full cycle of growth before it can be born fully developed so that it can function perfectly in this life. Based on that example, I think it is the same for the soul. It needs to fulfill its destiny completely, in order to progress in its next existence."

"Wonderful explanation Dr. Einstein. Now I think I also understand how the brain plays a vital role in human development. The thought occurred to me that I could perceive the soul in more simple terms by using an analogy: compare the body to a power station and your brain to a lamp; you can liken your soul to a powerful light bulb that is attached to a huge battery-like device. The power station provides the lamp with its energy that in turn makes the bulb glow continuously, while at the same time recharging the battery. Of course, without the power source, the lamp cannot function. Moreover, your lamp, your bulb and your storage battery are unique to you and to no one else. When your body dies, the power station shuts off and no longer gives its energy. So your bulb, with its battery, the kind that never burns out, needs to find a new source to plug into. What happens next is that your bulb will now have to rely on a more universal power source, such as, for example, the energy from the sun. Don't get this wrong, though. When the bulb with its charged storage battery (your soul) detaches from your lamp (your brain), it is a huge mass of energy, now in a state of equilibrium. This new journey that your bulb and its stored energy is embarking upon (your soul with its stored knowledge) will be made easier, based on what you've learned in your life and how you have applied what you learned. And the more you have learned the better, because within that experience is embedded the roadmap to your new energy source (God). If there are pieces of the roadmap missing, it will make your journey that much more arduous and unpleasant.

Einstein continuous "That is a good analogy Jack. I want to introduce you to a wonderful story-teller—one who will use his talent to help you understand better about the journey of life from beginning to end. This is important in our conversation about life and energy. Remember that in my talk about relativity, I mentioned that light is energy, and that it acts as a wave as well as a particle? I trust that I don't need to explain to you again that light bends because of gravity and that this proves that light has mass and is also therefore a particle. Are you with me? Well, the very fact that you're able to think proves that your thoughts are observable. They can be seen as waves using a device known as an MRI, or magnetic resonance imaging machine, which can scan the brain in real time. These vibrating waves, of different frequencies, shorter waves for the higher frequencies and longer waves for the lower frequencies reflect the activity of your brain.

"Do you understand? Just nod Jack, so I know you're still awake! Now, not only are these thoughts of yours actually waves of energy, you're also able to think in a very special way that is called 'rationally;' as far as we know, we humans are the only species equipped with the capacity to reason. And so all these rational thoughts are believed by some, such as the psychiatrist Karl Jung to be contained in what he called the 'universal human subconscious.'"

I am overwhelmed by this barrage of ideas and ask, "How do you know all this Dr. Einstein?"

He replies modestly, "mostly through observation, my dear boy. We scientists are trained to observe the different phenomena and draw conclusions based on our observations. Some conclusions are provable through mathematical formulae, and if proven correct become laws. If they cannot be proven, they are often called theories, which can later on become laws once they are proven to be correct. And as scientists, we also make use of the findings of other researchers such as Dr. Jung who, by the way, originally came up with the idea of the

77

'universal subconscious.' As a result, other scientists can build on these theories and come up with their own.

So let's get back to my original point about your soul; as I mentioned before, once the body dies, the rational soul exits the body, as a mass of energy, and continues from this bodily existence to the next existence, intact, with all that it has learned here on earth. The knowledge that is gathered by your rational soul becomes a part of the universal pool of knowledge. This knowledge is pooled with all the other knowledge from all other souls and that then represents the common pool of all the knowledge that Dr. Jung calls the 'universal subconscious.' The knowledge is available to all souls."

I hesitate. "Before we go on, may I ask a question about what happens when a newborn dies at birth or shortly thereafter? What happens to that soul?"

Einstein turns to Dr. Jung and asks him "What do you have to say about this question?"

Jung replies. "A soul enters into this life *tabula rasa*, that is, like a blank slate without prior knowledge, except for what I have termed as the 'universal subconscious.' The universal knowledge although it is available is of no use to you until you access it, either consciously or unconsciously. This means that nothing about this life has yet been inscribed in its soul. The baby's soul is as pure as God's white light. If at any point during its early life the baby dies, it goes straight to 'heaven,' because nothing from this physical life has made any impression upon its soul. God has given babies and infants a free pass into heaven. Does that answer your question Jack?"

"Yes, I think it does. Thank you."

"And now, I want to introduce you to our wonderful story teller, Aesop."

PART 7: THE STORIES OF LIFE ARE

NEVER FINISHED

"Hello Jack. My name is Aesop. I must say that these scientific types sure go on don't they? So now I want you to sit back, relax and enjoy a story of life I am about to tell you.

"By the way, it's a funny thing about knowledge. Remember, how Einstein said that we're all born—our soul that is—with all the knowledge already discovered built into our subconscious. That's nice, you say. But ask yourself this question: Why is it that until you are taught anything by your parents or your teachers, that you have none of this knowledge, even though some say that it is

81

within us? That is indeed a perplexing thought! But also how all those things we need for the survival of the physical body automatically kicks in to maintain life— things like the beating of your heart or how you "know" to breathe. But I truly can't understand why all the other stuff, which your physical body does not readily need is not accessible, until somebody unlocks your door of knowledge."

"But it gets better, Jack. What would you say if I told you that all the knowledge not yet discovered by anyone, resides within you. How do you like that?"

"OK, now I am intrigued. Tell me more. Why do we have to learn more? Why is it important that we must continually upgrade what we know?"

"Some people know the secret of telling stories. They know that you always want the listener to want more. In other words, the story is never finished. So it is with the story of life, death and redemption. It is never finished. It is cumulative, progressive and linear. In other words, you cannot skip any part of the story, you must listen to it in its entirety. It would be rather dull if the story of life was complete, with nothing more to add. So I prefer to think that the end of one life story is the jumping off point to a new one.

My stories about life are called fables. I used animals to represent people. And each story has a moral. Because knowledge is cumulative, the capacity to absorb new ideas always exists. So it is that storytellers like myself know that I can increase the complexity of the story by adding components that might not have been understood fifty years earlier. I think one must adapt stories to the time in which you live. I'm going to tell you a story, but let me preface it by asking you to imagine what I tell you in your mind's eye. If I told you a story that takes place in the year 1835 about a train, your brain would immediately see an image of a steam locomotive—cumbersome and not very streamlined. But if you think of a locomotive today, right away you picture a sleek machine, no longer powered by steam, superfast and efficient. Now if you think about how the world has changed over the last two thousand years, you can appreciate how you and I need to adapt to the needs of the world. There are now 7 billion people on earth. So we need to change our attitude from one of taking care of the people we know and expand our awareness to the ones we don't know. That is the change we all need to make. We have cultivated a greater capacity that includes the needs of all the peoples in the world, no matter where they are, no matter whether we know them or not. That is why I say that the story never ends, it merely changes with a growing awareness that the story now includes all the world's people. We need to cultivate new habits, and virtues we may not have possessed before, such as empathy for the plight of all, no matter where they are. That is why our knowledge needs to expand and we continue to learn. Get it?" Awareness is the key.

"But I promised you a story and here it is:

The Ant and the Chrysalis

An Ant nimbly running about in the sunshine in search of food came across a Chrysalis that was very near its time of change. The Chrysalis moved its tail, and thus attracted the attention of the Ant, who then saw for the first time that it was alive. "Poor, pitiable animal!" cried the Ant disdainfully. "What a sad fate is yours! While I can run hither and thither, at my pleasure, and, if I wish, ascend the tallest tree, you lie imprisoned here in your shell, with power only to move a joint or two of your scaly tail." The Chrysalis heard all this, but did not try to make any reply. A few days after, when the Ant passed that way again, nothing but the shell remained. Wondering what had become of its contents, he felt himself suddenly shaded and fanned by the gorgeous wings of a beautiful Butterfly. "Behold in me," said the Butterfly, "your much-pitied friend! Boast now of your powers to run and climb as long as you can get me to listen." So saying, the Butterfly rose in the air, and, borne along and aloft on the summer breeze, was soon lost to the sight of the Ant forever.

"So," Aesop explained, "the moral of the story is that things are not always as they seem. It is important to observe and learn your entire life. Thus will the soul be empowered to attain its ultimate destiny.

"But Aesop," I protest, "how do you know that the collective knowledge, as you call it, is not lost to the collective humanity that follows?"

"Well Jack, I don't know the answer to that. But I do know that since we are smarter today as a species, it seems that newborn souls start out their existence from a more evolved, more intelligent vantage point, with knowledge that seems to be built in. The soul has an unlimited capacity to learn, adapt and evolve so that the essence of its existence is continually pushed to a higher level of cognition. I agree with Einstein that the laws of thermodynamics that apply to everything in the universe apply equally to the human being. Let me refer you, once again to Dr. Jung, whom you met earlier. He can certainly shed more light on human consciousness, its characteristics, its quirks and quarks. Jung, as you know, was a contemporary of. Sigmund Freud, whom you also met. Like Freud, Jung was considered one of the pioneers of psychoanalysis and he has some interesting theories about human conscious and unconscious. But he also maintains that there exists a universal unconsciousness, what you refer to as the universal subconscious."

Intuition does not yield all the answers

"Hello again, Jack. I'm addressing you, including your imagination that seems rather opinionated about things. You are quite intuitive. But intuition only gets you so far. So I'm happy to return to shed more light on some of the ideas that you are struggling with, such as the existence of a rational soul and its ultimate destination. Dr. Einstein is quite right about the laws of thermodynamics, and if I can recall from Physics 101, the first and second laws rule all of life. The first law tells us that energy in the universe is constant. You cannot add to it or take away from it. It just changes form. But whatever there is that's all there is.

"The second law, entropy, is the one we'll explore because of the cause and effect relationship with the rational soul.

"Jack, the very proof of bodily life on earth is in the body's continuous and uninterrupted energy flow. As long as there is energy flow there is life. If energy flow stops, life is no longer sustainable. This continuous energy I refer to is the energy flow of your brain and your heart, the continuous interaction between all parts within your brain. It's all vitally important of course. However, if we could isolate the functioning of the parts in the brain that help in the education of the rational soul, it seems that rational thought is first processed in the left side of the brain, the side that deals with logic. But it is the continuous interaction between both hemispheres of the brain that produces the energy necessary for the education of the soul, as this involves millions upon millions of brain impulses, such as the understanding of beauty in all things, colours, hues, shapes, and so on. As long as this interaction continues, rational consciousness, and therefore life, continues. When the brain stops, we are considered clinically dead. The question you must ask yourself now is: where did the energy go? It did not disappear. Or did it? It can't just have vanished or been destroyed. No, the correct answer is that according to the law of entropy the soul is now in a state of equilibrium and has left the body with its life's experiences embedded. It no longer requires the brain. It just means that the soul is in search of its new destination."

I'm excited to hear this. But suddenly, Aesop appears again and says, "Hi Jack, I'm back! Didn't I tell you the story would get interesting? Let's continue with an imagined train voyage: the train passes many stations and picks up passenger cars and drops some off along the way. Remember that your soul can only travel this life's journey while a passenger in your own railway car (the body). And it's also a one-way journey. Along the way, your private passenger car makes many stops. During these stops, other private cars join your journey, and although they are private, they will interact with your car. You get to meet the passengers in the common car of the train where you socialize, play, learn and couple, to ensure the continued survival of the species. It's an important place during your journey, for it is here that you can learn and put into practice the virtues of life, such as love, compassion, service, justice, kindness, and so on. These virtues identify who we are and it is the learning and application of these virtues that causes us to leave an indelible mark on the book of humanity.

Aesop continues, "when your train has reached its final destination, your soul disembarks from your railway car and takes its flight into the universe. The soul's personality remains complete, with its knowledge intact, and joins other souls on its journey towards its permanent destination, the center of its attraction, that which prepared it for its earthly existence, the one many call God."

"Wait a minute!" I interject. "Something does not jive here. You talk about your body as a passenger car and your soul as the passenger of the car, but you do not explain the role of the locomotive that is pulling the passenger car. Therefore, I think your analogy, although it is elegant, is flawed. My question is: Who or what is the train? The other question I want to ask: The journey goes from where to where?"

Aesop patiently asks, "what do you think Jack? "

"I don't know," I reply cautiously. "If I knew, I wouldn't ask the question, would I?"

Still endlessly patient, Aesop says, "Jack, you're taking the easy way out. Remember that we're talking about an analogy here. It is a way to explain the unexplainable by putting it in terms that we might understand. So think again."

"OK, if we're talking about an imaginary train and an imaginary journey I would think that the locomotive must be time. And since we are traveling in time, the journey is the passage of time, right?"

Aesop laughs and says, "I'm proud of you Jack. That's exactly what my story is about. I knew you'd get it."

"Thanks for the compliment, but what still puzzles me is the idea that the train makes stops along the way and from time to time changes direction. What is that all about?"

"It's called free will, my dear Jack. You are the one that causes your passenger car to change directions. Perhaps Dr. Jung can assist here."

Your soul is unique

"Hi Jack. Let me tell you a little more about your soul. The soul is characterized by its uniqueness and its interrelationship with other souls; yet, at the same time, it is independent of other souls. Each soul has an arms-length kinship with other souls, but all have a common responsibility for the betterment of the whole. And so the journey your soul undertakes is under your control and unique and completely independent from the journey of all other souls.

"So this is what you've learned thus far, Jack:_Your soul has both a purpose and a destiny; a journey and a destination. The 'birth' and education of your soul starts at conception. It starts its existence as a blank slate, but at the same time it has embedded within it the sum total of all knowledge, both known (discovered) and unknown (not yet discovered). Your soul also possesses rationality in this existence. This is a significant characteristic of the progressive nature of evolution and of an everlasting existence. Thus, it is here, in this life, that our consciousness is slowed down enough to let us observe and learn. It is also the only way that the individual soul can learn. From the very fact that it has a reasoned existence within the body, it becomes a witness to knowledge and a participant in the gradual development of the universal knowledge base. It seems that here-and-now is the only opportunity for the soul to play such a participatory role in its own perfecting.

Jung continues, "we are enabled, in this lifetime, to contribute to the overall well-being of the 'Universal Soul,' while simultaneously taking responsibility for the education of our own. To measure the progress of our soul, we need the constraints of our limited physical existence and its relative slow motion, so that we can perceive, observe and quantify our acquired knowledge. As a purposeful, created form we must determine whether we will receive a passing grade for entry into our everlasting journey towards the light of creation.

PART 8: BURNING QUESTIONS

After all these conversations, I still find myself asking three burning questions: how much of what I have learned is usable in my next existence? How am I applying what I've learned in some positive way to the process for the common good of an evolving humanity? And finally, how much of what I have learned, solely for the gratification of my human curiosity, is of any use in my next existence?

A thousand names for the same destination

I am convinced that the interaction we will have with other souls in our next existence is strictly spiritual. If we have not learned to speak that spiritual language in our bodily existence, we will not be able to communicate with other souls. The language of the soul is cast in positive terms. There are no "negatives" in the next life. One either knows something or one does not. This may sound simple but it is not.

Imagine that you did not learn the skills for communication in the next life. When you get there it will be very difficult, if not impossible, to reach your goal, which is the contemplation of God, The Eternal light, the life Force, Nirvana or whatever other name you choose to call the object of your soul's adoration. There are at least a thousand names for the same destination.

Thus it is here, in this physical life, that we learn the language of the soul. That is the purpose of being here. The language is not French or English or German; no, it is a spiritual language that is learned through the acquisition of knowledge and the application of that acquired knowledge in the form of good deeds, performed for the common good. Progress towards the Light, in the next life, is mitigated by not having performed good deeds in this life. It's like a scorecard, with each good deed accounting for a goal in favour of the progress of your soul, with the lack of such a good deed as a missed goal. By the way, you cannot fool the system by using good deeds as a way into "heaven" if these deeds are not done with genuine love in your heart for your fellow beings and a genuine desire to be of service. Good news though, your job, no matter what it is, is to be of service to your fellow human beings. Service counts as a good deed.

Most importantly, without the application of what we have learned in this present life, this knowledge is of limited use. For it is in our ability to use what we've learned that gives our souls purpose and meaning and is a guide that indicates that we are on the right spiritual path.

I believe that there have been and will continue to be among us enlightened Beings, the recipients of Divine Knowledge directly from God. They are spiritual guides for each of us who let us assess what we've learned from them and what we've used of this knowledge for the overall good of humanity. The knowledge of these Holy Spirits encompasses all of the universal knowledge, past, present and future. However, based on our capacity to understand, they offer knowledge that is based on God's progressive revelation to man. They are the wellsprings of knowledge, inspired to help us along in our progress towards reaching the goal of our desire. It is vitally important to deepen on their Messages.

Knowledge solely for the purpose of self-gratification does not aid the soul's progress, unless this knowledge directly contributes to the wellbeing of oneself and others. One can think of medical discoveries, such as a cure for cancer or the common cold, etc. However, a new recipe for eggplant parmesan or a new mixed drink, that gets you drunk without a hangover does not count for anything.

In the last analysis, we're all only tiny particles in the cosmos, each one of us with a mission to contribute in some measure to an ever-evolving humanity. The same rules of birth, growth and decay apply to us, as they do to everything else in the universe. Nothing ever gets lost or disappears, but merely changes from one form to another. All of us are ultimately just energy.

So, I say to myself, Jack, this then is your destiny and purpose in the universe. The education of my soul is no trivial or part-time task and the commitment I make towards it will be reflected in the soul that remains once I've left this earthly realm.

I feel more enlightened at this point and have the distinct feeling that I have learned a lot. But I still have questions to ask. For example, if this progressive evolution is important for the progress of man, why have we been given free will?

The dilemma of free will

Finally, I have come to understand that our souls seem to be part of one great rational entity and that we have been endowed with intelligence and the ability to make choices. If it were otherwise, our ability to gather and understand knowledge and use it to good ends would be seriously impaired.

PART 9: MEDITATION IS

IMPORTANT

I ask Dr. Deepak, "is meditation important to the progress of the soul?"

"Yes Jack it is. We should devote regular time to meditation and the way we can best accomplish that state is to let go of the clamour of our left brain. Things such as: I forgot to bring home a gallon of milk; or, I should have given my boss a piece of my mind for the way he treats me. These are definitely an impediment to meditation. We should instead concentrate on the right side of the brain for its ability to observe calmness and serenity. You can do this by likening yourself to a pool of water that expands

95

further and further and you follow it as it merges with other pools and eventually reaches the sea, where all the water merges. Your left brain, your brain's strident side, will attempt to pull you back because it wants answers and sets boundaries. Of course, your left side is important, because your life's experience and knowledge gathered here could not have been accomplished without the use of logic and, without it, your progression into the next life would be severely hampered. We need the logical and sequential side to put what we've learned in the proper order, so that the result and the experiences of what we've gathered here remains embedded as the sum total of all the knowledge that we take with us on our next journey. The left brain activity ceases in the next existence, because our journey is no longer constrained by time and space.

"But meditation, continues Dr. Deepak, "means focusing and quieting your brain. It lets you reach a higher level of passive awareness and inner calm. And, by the way, it is possible to meditate anywhere. It is the practice of meditation that allows you to perfect the process so that you can do it anytime and anywhere."

"Deepak I must say that I have great difficulty meditating. My thinking is confused and disconnected, so meditation is something I have not yet mastered. I guess it requires practice. I appreciate the fact that it is one way to get in touch with my inner self and instinctively feel that it is somehow linked to my soul. But how can I know what I need to meditate about in order for my soul to reach its ultimate destination?"

"Jack, it is every person's responsibility to gather knowledge for the advancement of his own eternal soul and all other souls as well, for the improvement of human destiny. It is a forward-moving awareness through our presence here that forces us to unravel the mysteries of our existence. The more we can connect to the mysteries of this present existence the better we are able to navigate the flow of life itself. So it is a multifunctional reality. I mean to say that by advancing the education of our own soul, we can simultaneously influence the progress of mankind's common destiny, since they are inextricably linked. To distance ourselves from this social responsibility—that is, the knowledge and application of good deeds for the common good—is to detach ourselves from the reality of our very birth into this world. We cannot deny that we all spring from a single source. Therefore, we need to find the common thread that binds us together. It is a continuous, search that is based on the progressive discovery of the human capacity, while utilizing that which we have already uncovered. We do have control, to a certain extent, over our own brain. But the development of the human brain is anchored to a strong social connect that is characteristic in Western society and thus to humanity's irresistible progression towards a more perfect world. Continually seeking to find truth and relevance allows us a glimpse into the future. It develops our capacity to see humanity improving as it advances, making mistakes along the way, but also bettering itself by learning from those mistakes. The miracle of human existence is in its capacity to evolve into a more perfect image of its former self. This means that the being of today, informed as it is with the cumulative knowledge of us all, has the capacity for the betterment of the human lot. To be sure, there are encumbrances that make us stray, such as selfishness, self-aggrandizement and the unending pursuit of material gain. But in the end, we must all realize that for each one of us it is about becoming better each day than we were the previous day. To sum it all up: the information that is essential to attaining our goal to reach the "Eternal Light"—God, or Heaven, or whatever you chose to call the "hereafter"—is the sum total of knowledge from your lifetime of living here on this earth, shaped in part by all the information from the ever-advancing society in which you lived."

"Great," I say, still a little perplexed. "I'm afraid I need some more explanation."

"Well, do you recall that we talked about your learning room and your Mother saying to you: 'Never stop learning Jackie?' Remember that?"

"Yes, I do."

"Good, because besides using what you learn in this life for practical applied use, that same knowledge is also essential in your next life to continue your journey. This knowledge also automatically includes all the accumulated information from humanity's past. All human beings, as stakeholders, have a vested interest to participate in the gathering of knowledge that thrusts humanity along on its quest for a kinder, gentler, better and more just world. In other words, Jack, you cannot be a mere spectator. Moreover, you cannot rely on information that was selectively fed to you by the denizens of religion, without verifying that what you have been taught as spiritual verities is the relevant spiritual truth from God's Progressive Revelation to an ever evolving, wiser humanity. Adhering to dogma and ritual expressions of spirituality, no matter how beautiful and ornate they are, simply won't get you to your destination. It has been said that God's Words have as many meanings as there are atoms in the universe. It is vitally important you discover as many as you can and that takes a lot of learning.

"And by the way, the only thing that matters is the way you applied the spiritual or practical knowledge you gained in this life for the maturation of your rational soul and its progress in the world hereafter. The fact that you accumulated a lot of wealth along the way, or bought yourself a villa in the south of France or a ten million dollar brownstone in New York does not count for anything in your next existence; unless, of course, you used your wealth to help others. Financial wealth has no value in heaven.

"And how do I know all this?" Deepak suddenly asks rhetorically. "Because I have drawn upon the knowledge and spiritual wisdom of people that are far wiser than I am."

PART 10: MY EXPLANATION OF THE "THEORY OF EVERYTHING"

"Hi, Jack. My name is William Blake, the poet. May I put in my two cents-worth? I wrote the *Auguries of Innocence* sometime around 1763: 'To see a world in a grain of sand, And a heaven in a wild flower, Hold infinity in the palm of your hand, And eternity in an hour....'

"If you listen carefully, you can hear God's voice telling the story of the birth of the universe. It has no degrees of separation. Jack, do you sense the sameness in all things from this poem? Everything in God's world of creation, including us, conforms to all of God's rules about birth, life and the hereafter. We're all related and we're all an

101

integral part of the greater whole. We are all connected and whatever it is that we inherit at conception we are responsible to educate. We are therefore subservient, like everything else, to God's laws and the rules of integration and disintegration."

"Mr. Blake, it's nice to meet you and I love your poem. And I am interested in your commentary about life. But what do you mean by 'integration and disintegration'?"

"That's an odd question Jack. Obviously my poetry resonated well since you quoted it in the same context as your exploration into the theory that explains everything. So why do you ask this question?"

"Well, as I understand it, life begins at birth and ends with death. These are pretty finite events, so how do integration and disintegration relate to birth and death?"

"Well, let me see how I can answer your question. Integration consists of the bonding of different elements that occurs through what many believe to be the Divine Will. Others think it to be the result of chance. These compound elements form a strong bond that results in the 'birth' of complex life forms. Disintegration is the reverse procedure of that process and results in the 'death' and decomposition of that complex organism."

"That's a pretty complicated answer for something that we've come to accept as a simple event. But I do have another question: You were born in the 1700s, when enlightenment thinking was already almost a century old. How do your poetry and your art reflect your views on philosophy and religion? How different are they from those of Isaac Newton or John Locke, for example?"

The changeless face of God

"My ideas about life and truth are rooted in the belief that the order in the universe—and therefore the social order—is pretty much preordained by God. Therefore, we should give ourselves over to the idea that what we need to do is look after one another. Enlightenment or the Age of Reason, as it was often called, was popular in my time. Isaac Newton and John Locke were also a part of the new-enlightened thinking and they were champions of this new age. However, in contrast to my views, Newton's laws cast the world in terms of natural laws beyond any spiritual force. John Locke held that people had the right to challenge a government that did not protect the natural rights of life, liberty and property. My commentary views life through the lens of spirituality and demonstrates that there are spiritual solutions to political problems. At the same time of heightened awareness, people were starting to question the existence of a God who on the one hand had the power to send man into hell if He so wished and on the other empower a tyrant as king. These ideas would change the face of Europe forever. My views on enlightenment, as it relates to explaining everything, are important because they relate everything to a process that is governed by a higher entity. Existence is organic and it changes to meet the exigencies of the moment. What remains changeless is the face of God.

"The mystery lies in trying to comprehend the union of simple elements into complex structures. So what we need to do in life is attempt to understand the complexity that explains this process. There is, first of all, a process of attraction. This attraction is the same for all elements, but is identified by many different words that describe its special chameleon-like ability to cast life, love, unity,

103

adaptability…and so on into meaningful elements. For example, the attraction between two beings is demonstrated by their love for one another. This then causes these beings to come together and couple. The union then produces offspring, thus furthering the endless process. Adaptability means that things evolve based on the needs of the time. Words can explain the universality of the wonder of all existence, but not in an efficient way. Understanding lies not in the ability to deconstruct the words into simpler meanings, but reflects the attempt to understand the complexity of the word in its entirety, just as the word 'love' loses its meaning if you deconstruct it into simpler parts, since the complexity of the word is what love means. So it is with all existence: the single word, just like the single oak seed, has no real meaning until it has grown into the mighty oak tree, The single human cell cannot be seen in its miraculous entirety until it is born, even though, as a single cell, it contains a complete and accurate rendering of its ultimate form, right down to the minutest details. This is the special wonder of creation: We're all destined to do what we are meant to do. In the vegetable kingdom, this means growing into what the vegetable is meant to become: a squash seed becomes a squash plant that grows squash; an apple seed becomes an apple tree, and so on. Then in the animal kingdom, the lower animals, in addition to having the capacity to grow, also possess the capacity to act: the primal impulse of a hungry lion compels him to kill another animal in order to survive. It's built into its DNA and it does so instinctively. But the higher animal, the human being, has all the same capacities, growth, instinctive and intuitive thinking, and more importantly, the very quality that sets us apart from the lower animals, rational thought."

"What is rational thought?" I ask. "Why must we be witness to the unfoldment of the universe? Why can't it just evolve without my being a witness to it? What can I do, even as I witness some of its intricacies? Without knowing why, it seems purposeless. We have no control over what happens, even if we know, right?"

"Well," Blake answers, "rational thought is the ability to use logic to figure something out or the ability to reason and acquire knowledge. Moreover, we have free will to choose our actions. The cycles of birth, death and decomposition are preordained; we cannot control them; we are part of the eternal loop."

"But I'm running out of steam answering all your questions! So let me bring Aristotle in on this issue. I know that many things he has said resonate well with you. Hopefully, he can shed more light on the complex questions you are asking!"

"Hello, Jack. Aristotle here. Remember what I wrote about metaphysical knowledge? Metaphysics implies that something is what it is and that no further explanations can be had at this time in your existence. Nevertheless there are reasons why we have been given rational thought and one of them is that, for whatever reason, we must bear witness to the endless unfoldment of the universe. Why that is, we don't know. What we do know is that without man's witness there is no knowledge, there is only existence. In the universe this Force that is in control of all things is just like the conductor of the greatest orchestra in creation, directing the symphony of life and death. It is surely a grand theme. The soul that you were given needs knowledge. You think you know why. You will surely know the reason why after you pass from this existence into the next. The best analogy for understanding the relationship between this life and the next is that of the baby in the womb. The baby is growing all its appendages, arms and legs to move, nose, eyes and ears to see, smell and hear, right? But it has absolutely no use for these in the womb. The reason that these are needed becomes abundantly clear when it is born into this life."

I am growing impatient with Aristotle's explanations and reply, "Why should I care how the world of existence evolves? What possible difference does it make whether I know this or not?"

"Be patient, Jack. Today, you may believe that God exists but you do not know for sure. The only way that you will know for sure is when in the next existence you have your developed spiritual eyes with which to see Him. These are the very spiritual eyes that you developed in this lifetime. These eyes will allow you to be in His presence without being blinded by the Light. So you see; that is your mission in *this* life. You will have to become a lot smarter on a spiritual level than you are now or else you won't be able to perceive him in your state of ignorance!

But whether or not you believe in God, you must admit that there is something far greater than us at work in our earthly existence and that it seems to control the order of things. So, if we agree on that, we'll call it—for lack of a better definition—the 'God' universe. And even though it is all around us and within us, it manifests itself as pure energy, it remains completely invisible to us, except that we know that it has to do with the expansion of a super-dense energy source. We know that this source exploded into a myriad of sub component parts of matter and energy. We, of course, are an integral part in this cosmic soup. Not understanding the whole because of the parts is a plight that we've been attempting to resolve in order to gain an understanding of why it is that we have been created in this way. This little bit of energy that we call our own is given to us so that we can alter it, make it better, so to speak, give it knowledge, so that it can eventually have enough wisdom to become part of an entity we assume exists, but of which we know very little. This is the theory of the very large, distinct and separate, but nevertheless most confounding thing that insistently takes centre-stage in our consciousness.

Albert Einstein and his colleagues spent much of their lives researching and developing theories that attempt to explain precisely this. We've always struggled with the concept of defining what or who God is. The inevitable answer we arrive at is that God is unknowable. In the world of energy there is no time, just energy. There is no logic at work here and there is no fast forward or reverse, night or day, no seasons, no good or bad, just energy. We can't explain it; all we can do is think it. That's all we really know. And if God wills it, He appoints certain beings—we call them Messengers or Prophets of God and He imbues them with the very qualities that reflect His attributes. Thus, He educates us through them. These Beings are visible to us and our task is to emulate them so that we can become like them. That is the mission of every soul that is born into this existence, and this is a necessary way-station for learning. Without this stop in our everlasting existence, we are unable to participate in the next stage of existence, that is, the merging of all souls with God. It is at once a never-ending process and one that improves the quality and quantity of the knowledge each soul yields to this common Energy. The cycle is endless. And it is this never-ending cycle that explains everything in existence.

PART 11: THE ROOM OF

DIMENSIONS

"Hey, there is no knob on this door, just a round circle where the knob should be!"

A voice from inside the rooms booms out at me: "Veffer, I told you before: if you're going to draw pictures you must understand the three dimensions. What are they?"

There is no mistaking that voice. Every time I hear it my hair stands on end. It is the dreaded voice of Bill Williams, my Grade Six art teacher.

"Well," I mumble, "one dimension is height; then there is width, and depth, the one I'm always having trouble drawing."

"That's why you can't get in the room. If you draw the lines so they run away from you can draw the illusion of depth."

"I could never master it, Mr. Williams. Let me try it again by drawing this door. Yes. I think I've got it now, Sir."

"Good. Now you can see the doorknob and come into the room of dimensions. There are other things I must show you in this room."

I enter the room and hesitate at the entrance. Mr. Williams does not like me much, ever since I told him I did not like Vincent Van Gogh paintings, his hero.

"Well don't just stand there, boy. I want you to meet someone. This gray haired gentleman with me is Albert Einstein." I heave a sigh of relief, since I know Mr. Einstein well.

Einstein winks at me knowingly and asks, "Did you ever hear of my theory of relativity, Mr. Veffer."

"I have, sir, although I must admit that I'm not quite sure how it works, I know the words to explain the theory."

"That's wonderful!" he says. "Well let me try to explain it to you so you can understand it. It involves another dimension. And this is one you can't draw on paper, he says, chuckling at his own joke. "It is has to do with time and I call it the Fourth Dimension."

I have trouble understanding what Einstein is saying, perhaps because he speaks English with a heavy German accent; or maybe I'm just too stupid to understand.

"Pay attention, Mr. Veffer. You will eventually understand it. I will put you in a spacecraft that will move at a speed of 200,000 km per second. I'll send you on a trip to outer space and back. Mr. Williams and I will remain here and wait for your return. Make sure you keep track of the time you spend. Mark the days on the calendar you have on board."

"But Mr. Einstein, do I have to go by myself? Why can't you come with me?"

"Mr. Veffer, remember that this is *your* mansion of reality, *your* experience, not ours. All I'm here for is to teach you things. You must learn and test what you've learned to be true or false. Goodbye, Mr. Veffer. Godspeed! We'll see you back in a few years."

I close my eyes as my spaceship blasts off into outer space. At the dizzying speed of 200,000 km per second, the spaceship travels to Mars and beyond. It then circles another planet, I don't know which one, and then roars back to earth. I keep careful track of the time as Einstein has instructed. Finally, I return to earth and arrive at my mansion exactly ten days after I blasted off. In the meantime, I think to myself, Einstein and Mr. Williams seem to have gotten very old in those ten days. I say nothing to them, because I don't want to upset them, but it seems that they really haven't taken very good care of themselves!

"Do you notice anything unusual about Mr. Williams?" Mr. Einstein asks me as he sees me emerge from the spaceship.

"Not really," I reply sheepishly.

"Come on now, Jack. Be honest. This was an experiment. Can't you see that he has aged quite a lot, while you barely aged at all? He is exactly 50 years older than when you left, while you aged only a few days. You've experienced a phenomenon known as time dilation. Time has been running much slower for you while you traveled in the fast-moving spacecraft than it has for him. The faster you move the slower time moves and the slower you move the faster time moves. That young Mr. Veffer is my Theory of Relativity. Do you get it now?

"Yes, thank you Mr. Einstein. But did I have to waste ten days of my life finding this out. Couldn't you just have explained it to me? I would have understood."

"A picture's worth a thousand words and action is worth ten thousand words, my boy. Maybe this will give you food for thought and maybe you'll discover another dimension," he says, as he waves goodbye and takes off on his bicycle, his snowy white hair blowing in the breeze.

Since he mentioned a new dimension, I had some time to think about that while I was on the space craft and I realize that many people who have come before me have gathered knowledge. This knowledge actually remains with us and is stored up in a place of universal consciousness. This knowledge is there for all to use and is stored somewhere, as I already explained. I decided to name that place the Divine Dimension.

The room called "time"

"Dr. Jung I do understand that my brain is structured to operate between the functional and the aesthetic and that the different parts of the brain, logical and analog are indispensable to each other and always work in unison. But it seems to me that the intensity of these brain functions varies widely, depending upon the exigencies of the moment; sometimes the functionality operates almost exclusively to the detriment of the romantic side, and vice versa, and often points somewhere in between. Can you explain why it is that our thinking works in that way? Are we driven by circumstance rather than by design? Is the moment more strident than planning? Is the human condition preordained or do we control our destiny?"

"These are deep and complex questions, Jack. I will need some help from other experts to address them. As a psychoanalyst, I can talk to your questions that have to do with the brain and human behaviour. When it comes to questions about destiny and free will or something in between destiny and free will, we'll need to travel to the Time room in your mansion and we'll need to enlist the help of one who has made a lifelong study of time, Dr. Stephen Hawking."

"Hi Jack, Stephen here. I'll race you to your Time room. When you look way down the hall of your mansion, you'll see a door. You can barely see it from here, but trust me it's there. Let's see who can get there first. Ok? Ready, set, go!"

After a very long time and completely exhausted, I arrive at the door that has a sign that identifies it as the "time room." Hawking is already here, impatiently waiting for me.

"What took you so long boy?"

Somewhat insulted, I reply, "It's an awfully long way to travel from where I was. You're in a wheelchair, so how did you get here so fast?"

"Well, unlike you, I did not physically travel here in my wheelchair; that's much too slow and tiring. I used my mind to get here. It allows me to get wherever I want to go in an instant. So here we are."

"Dr. Hawking, where is Dr. Jung?"

"Dr. Jung is still in your psychoanalysis room, pondering the question of how he can heal the human condition in time. But he suspects all along that what ails the human mind is merely the perception of reality which cannot be changed in time, but only altered in the mind. That's why he decided not to accompany us on this journey. He is presently experimenting with mandalas. He calls his mandalas graphical representations of existence."

"Oh, yes I remember. Now what about my perception of reality being my reality."

"Very good, Jack, you are listening. Hopefully, we might be able to answer part of that question by opening the door to your Time room. Stand back while I carefully open it."

As the door opens, I feel an overpowering, all-encompassing burst of energy that nearly sucks me in. It surely would have, had Dr. Hawking not warned me to stand back.

"What in the world is that?" I ask, somewhat stunned.

"That, Jack, is time. It is energy that moves in all directions at once, through the entire energy spectrum and in all known frequencies. It moves so fast that all events, past, present and future coexist here. That is why, when you ask whether we affect the events in time or not, that the answer to that question is an emphatic yes and no, since all events already exist. There is no beginning and no end to it. We are part of it but we do not affect it. The events that you think will affect the outcome of time are, in reality, mere miniscule slices that in no way matter in the outcome of the predestined path of time. It is preordained by an entity that we believe exists but do not know anything about. It is not one that we can see at any rate. It is one that we are told came before everything and set the stage for our progressive evolution from stage to stage. It is our sense of reality that makes us think that we are affecting the destiny of time because our perception is our reality.

"A strange phenomenon about time is how we measure it. For that concept we can thank Einstein and Poincaré, who both claimed, unlike Newton, that time is not absolute, but relative. They forever fundamentally changed our concept of time and we know from Einstein's famous formula $E=MC2$ that time is measured as mass times the square root of the speed of light. Thus, we cannot separate time from space and can make time what we want it to be. By doing so, we believe that our interaction with it changes events. In effect, all we can do in time is affect a tiny strand of it and only that strand that we seem to occupy in space. It is but an exceedingly tiny and slowed-down

115

version of the fearsome energy we witnessed in your Time room. In other words, the entire energy stream of time is not accessible to us and interaction with the entire spectrum is thus impossible. In itself, that is significant, since it makes the interaction possible in a very large wave form, so large, in fact, that it slows time down enough that we can be a participant in it and be a witness to events, to perceive its cause and effect. The larger the time wave is, the slower time moves. It is the only occasion in our eternal existence that we are enabled not only to participate in the events of time, but also to play some part in the outcome, be it is infinitesimal.

That's the part that confounds us: what makes time slow down, so that it feels as if we're going through a gooey, sticky mass? What is the substance or particle that slows it down enabling us to have an observable and participatory vantage point? Furthermore, it is true that your own experiences of life and those that affect your life's progress are those of your own making. Let me ask you this question: Can you measure your impact on the outcome of time? Looking from the outside into your Time room, all that you can see is this tremendous energy without a beginning, middle or end, right? If you were to jump into this maelstrom and affect the outcome of time where do you think you'd start?"

"Is that a trick question?" I ask, rather surprised. "There does not seem to be a way to enter this room in a predetermined spot that you can call your own. It all looks the same to me."

"Right. There is no way. So the only way that we can go in is not by pulling at the entire energy stream, but by pulling away a tiny strand of this energy and interacting with it in some way. In that way, even though what you do and what you think affects only a miniscule part of the time energy stream. I hope that you now grasp that what you do is insignificant as it relates to the overall outcome. What has a virtual impact on the outcome is your ability to unravel some of the mysteries of existence, or your discovery for the cure of cancer, for example; these will affect a greater number and therefore leave an indelible mark in time. All that we can say about time is that it is what it is. Any moment in time that you think is a moment is just your way of trying to derive a sense of involvement with it."

"Do you mean to say that we have no impact on human destiny?"

"No we do have an impact, but not in the way you think. First of all, most of the major discoveries that are made which affect man's destiny and its fulfillment are already mapped out. In other words, these earthshaking, destiny-shaping occurrences are meant to happen and have an impact on the way human destiny is meant to play out. That is the predestination component of time. It would be strange, indeed, if they were meant to happen and didn't. It's like connecting the dots in the time map and all of a sudden another gate opens. But don't misunderstand what I'm telling you; those discoveries that help unravel the mysteries of the universe are exactly that, great and earthshaking. They do shape human destiny, since they were meant to happen, simply because all of time is already mapped out: past present and future."

"Dr. Hawking, I have to admit to you that what you have said makes no sense to me at all. What if Einstein had not made his discovery about relativity? Some of the advances in science and technology could not have been made and we would not have been able to use his theories as jumping off points for other great ideas and advances in science and technology."

Unfazed, as usual, Dr. Hawking continued. "That's exactly my point. They happened as they were meant to happen. It would have been unthinkable if they were meant to happen and didn't. It would have caused a paradox. You will be interested to know that the relativity of time allows for many different outcomes besides the one that you are experiencing. So it stands to reason that there exist parallel universes to this one where different outcomes are the result of what you alluded to. So if Einstein had not developed his theories, different outcomes would have resulted, but not in the same universe. In other words, what is meant to happen in the universe you experience will happen and no other results are possible.

"Finally, let me explain to you that your interaction with time and its subsequent results is based in frequencies and wavelength. It is your ability to operate on a set frequency in time that allows you to interact with other beings and things that operate in the same frequency range. For example, the time frequency length you operate in is very short; if you were flying a remote toy airplane or car, you would use a short micro-channel frequency to control these toys to control only that one toy and not affect things beyond their range. And so it is with time: at the micro-channel level, your impact is on the things and events surrounding you, but when it comes to larger events such as natural phenomena, such as earthquakes and tsunamis, your actions, no matter how heroic, cannot prevent these events from happening. There are billions upon billions of events in time that neither affect you nor change the course of your destiny, because the universe is just too huge; and also because they operate on a myriad of frequencies that are too short to affect you. However, even if these events did affect your life, their influence would be so infinitesimal, that you might not even know they happened. So in terms of cause and effect, your sphere of influence is finite and limited to things and people within your frequency range and dissipates into the limitless expanse of time and space."

Always anxious to relate the scientific to the spiritual, I ask, "Dr. Hawking, you say we marginally affect the outcome of time; but since we do have free will and can make choices that shape the future of humanity, do you think that we can affect events by making better choices, if we are more empathetic human beings for example?"

"Yes, I certainly do, Jack. Our mission and purpose during our sojourn here is to gather the knowledge and develop the capacity to set the stage for a more peaceful human existence, one that is based on principles of conduct that ennoble us. I believe that humanity is currently in a state of moral decay and that we have a most uncertain future. But remember what was said about multiple universes. This is your universe and the only one in which you can have an impact. And you can only exist and experience and see the results of your actions and those around you in your own universe. You'll probably ask me if there is a different and unique universe for every human being, right? The answer to that is yes, I think. But don't worry about that now; maybe you'll understand it one day, and maybe not. Just remember why you're here.

This then is your mission and the mission of everyone on earth for the progress of the collective soul and the achievement of your own soul's desire, that is to meet its Creator."

My head is reeling!

PART 12: DOING GOOD IN YOUR LIFE

Mr. Geyser, my teacher in religious studies, yells at me with a tone of exasperation in his voice: "Mr. Veffer the correct term is "doing well in life, not doing good in life."

"But sir, I meant it as "doing good deeds in life," so if you'll allow me to further explain my point on the education of the soul." I rather enjoy sparring with Mr. Geyser. Right now he's giving me the evil eye because he doesn't like to be contradicted.

"OK, Mr. Veffer, you may continue." he says reluctantly, in a tone of voice that betrays his displeasure.

"Thank you sir. As I was saying; Doing good is a necessary component for the education of one's eternal soul. Do you not agree that it is not only essential for the soul to gather knowledge, but that it is also important to put this knowledge to good use in the service of one's fellow human beings? And I believe that includes having a positive attitude, thinking good thoughts. So these two qualities, doing good and thinking good, help our rational souls to mature."

I seem to have taken Mr. Geyser by surprise and he asks, "What do you mean when you say the 'rational soul;' why don't you just call it the soul?"

"Well, sir," I reply, happy that he is now engaging in the conversation, "when I say rational I mean that we are guided by our intellect. We have the ability to reason and analyze. This rational behaviour is precisely what separates us from the other animals. They can only behave from instinct, experience and emotion, rather than deductive reasoning. As far as we know and are told so often, the soul lives on after death and it needs the continued ability to reason. That is why the rational soul goes on into another existence. There is a good reason for doing good however, because in the long run, doing good deeds and thinking good thoughts is beneficial to the soul and, more importantly, even releases those chemicals in the brain that have an overall therapeutic effect on the physical body and fight disease.

"So, please don't think that this 'good doing' implies having an ulterior motive. The act of doing good deeds becomes a way of life and is therefore an end in itself. Because the mind is the repository of all that we do and think, we have the opportunity, during our time on earth, to fill it with positive and goodly deeds that leave their indelible mark on the mind. But it is not a free pass into heaven! Rather, it facilitates the journey to heaven, because the pathway to heaven has been traced like a roadmap in the mind. It is a graphical roadmap that we will use as beacon towards the Eternal Light once we have departed from this earthly life."

"Well, Veffer, let's say that I accept the premise that the rational soul is on an eternal journey and that the two travel together. But there is also the little matter of the mind. You keep saying that the mind is the repository for the sum total of man's knowledge. What happens to the mind and all this knowledge? Does it go to waste?"

"No, sir, not at all! The rational soul also contains the mind with all its knowledge. They are inseparable."

Geyser is becoming a little exasperated with me and re-joins, "Let me play the devil's advocate here. Why do you think we should do good? After all, to most of us death is final and therefore it is of little or no concern to us what happens after we die."

"True," I reply, "but here's the rub: if your earthly life is filled with good as opposed to the absence of good, then and only then will you be enabled to discern the path to 'Heaven.' It's the only roadmap. Bad does provide you with the directions to that preordained place called Heaven. You can do bad things if you so choose, for we have been given freedom of choice. If you get away with it and gain an advantage in whatever tangible way that is meaningful to you—such as making money—I can tell you, it counts for nothing in the afterlife. We're all road builders in this life and these roads are for our own exclusive use. Hopefully, the road to travel will be completed when we pass from this earthly realm. Once we've constructed the road, it remains forever embedded in our mind. Since my soul is unique to me, I am the only ones responsible for its nurturing. So, in the end, the absence of good deeds tends to blot out the path. The soul loses its way and cannot move forward towards the Light. We can see the Light, but only from an excruciatingly great distance.

Certain practices, such as meditation and prayer can enlighten the soul to become more loving, nurturing, empathetic and altruistic. These are good qualities to have."

I look around the classroom for some reaction, a hint, perhaps, that someone has understood what I said. All I get are vacuous stares. Someone is trying to stifle a yawn. Nervously, I look at Mr. Geyser.

"Mr. Veffer," he begins, "obviously you've thought about this subject a great deal. It appears that you may be on to something. Well done, I say. Don't let it go to your head, though. After class I want to hear more of your ideas. So stay after class."

"Thank you, sir!" I say gratefully, feeling a little self-satisfied, but wondering what ammunition Mr. Geyser has in mind to demolish my views on the rational soul.

All the while I stay in my learning room. I could be out exploring other parts of my mansion. But the subject of the soul and its progress really intrigues me and curiosity keeps me here. When everyone is dismissed, I anxiously watch Mr. Geyser, as he busies himself stuffing test papers into his briefcase. Finally he looks up and says, "So, Mr. Veffer, tell me some more of your interesting ideas. I must say that I find your views on the soul intriguing. Do you really think that what we do here in this life has an impact in a life hereafter? Where did you come by these ideas?"

"Yes, sir, I do believe that. I have always been fascinated with the idea that human beings have an earthly destiny to fulfill. I believe that it is our destiny to take care of the soul given to us at conception. Even though each soul forms part of the greater "Universal Soul," it is uniquely the property and responsibility of its individual owner. Our mission here is to gather knowledge, so that we can educate the soul and, in tribute to our Fashioner (God), use that knowledge for the good of all. The knowledge thus used is the measure of humanity's advancing maturity. The evidence of whether mankind has reached its full maturity culminates in a world, in which there is no longer any strife or war, but everlasting peace and contentment."

"Jack, that is beautiful. How did you come to this realization?" he asks. And I'm aware that this is the first time that he called me by my first name.

"The thing is sir, that I have cultivated an uneasy belief in the existence of God. Throughout all time, God has educated humanity and continues to do so. This He does by appointing special individuals, some of whom may, in fact, be quite ordinary, but who, once they have been imbued with the Holy Spirit, become empowered with extraordinary insight. And it is these beings who

125

continually bring a fresh message for mankind with which God endows His chosen ones."

"How does one recognize these chosen ones of God?"

"They are recognizable by their qualities of noble character and behaviour and their superlative knowledge. Before their appointment, they may have been quite different, as in the case of Moses, who earlier was accused of murder and had a severe speech impediment. But after his transformation by God, he became the leader of his people, the Jews, gave them the Ten Commandments and made them a great nation. There was no mistaking him, since he announced his mission to the Jews. Of course, there were a great many people who did not believe him. Nevertheless, over time, it became undeniable that he was who he said he was. Other signs that were significant in the time that they occurred was the performance of great feats, such as the parting of the Red Sea, allowing the Jews to cross and preventing the Egyptians from pursuing them. They drowned when the sea engulfed them, when they too tried to cross.

The next one that we, in our Judaeo-Christian society, can readily identify is Jesus Christ. His appointment came in the midst of Jews, who fell under the yoke of a prideful hierarchy. They were heedless of some of Moses' messages, in particular the promise that someday a Messiah would appear. So they stopped looking for him and contented themselves with waiting until the Rabbinate, the ruling institution, eventually would tell them that He had come. This is a day that sadly has not yet come as far as the learned of the Jewish faith contend.

Jesus' message to the people was simple enough: he preached that everyone should 'love his neighbour.' Of course, there was more to his message than that. Meekness and patience were qualities that he demonstrated and therefore urged others to behave similarly. His simple message; dying for mankind's sins, was so important that he chose to be crucified for it rather than recant his beliefs. That measure is one by which man recognized Jesus' station and his faith spread like wildfire, such that millions accepted his message throughout the known world.

These consecutive messages from Moses and later Jesus were directed to a specific people for a specific time to remedy a specific malady. Not only were they consecutive messages, but also they were progressive in nature. God's messages become increasingly all encompassing, including ever greater portion of humanity. We became smarter and had a greater capacity to understand the concept of God's revelation that was progressive in nature and tailored to the specific needs of a maturing humanity."

By this point, Geyser was listening intently and asked, "as far as you know, Jack, can you say that there have been others in history, to whom God has given this capacity to see Him and receive a Divine Message from Him?"

"Yes, I believe so. History has already identified the major ones. They have been permanently recorded in the Holy Books of the great world religions, such as the Five Books of Moses (the Torah), and the New Testament, the testimony of the Apostles, Matthew, Mark, Luke and John and for the dispensation of Mohammad, the Koran. There are numerous others, less familiar to us in the Western world but nevertheless known to billions of people in the East."

"Jack, I must congratulate you. At such a young age—you're 15 now, right? —You're showing that you've given this subject a lot of thought. Although I don't agree with everything you said, I can respect your viewpoint. You might want to further your studies, once you graduate from high school, and go into religious studies, and develop further theories about the soul and the concepts of heaven and hell."

"Thank you, sir. I will certainly consider it."

PART 13: CONCLUSION

"Deepak, what will I ultimately be, if this is not my final form?"

"You are part of a process of events that will shape you to what you will become. You must appreciate, however, before I go any further with this explanation, that you and everyone else are a work in progress. You are part of a complex system in the universe that keeps evolving. That is why it is so difficult to actually comprehend who you really are. When you look at your life in this realm, you cannot fathom your end product; the parts of your life, more often than not, don't give you clues about your final destination. But we do know that as God-fearing beings, our mission in life comes from the guidance we receive from God's Messengers. We accept, only with firm faith, that if we are obedient to God's commands, we will become what we were meant to become and end in the place where we are meant to be. Since we are but one miniscule component in the ever-changing energy spectrum, it is impossible to conjecture from it what our end will look like. At any one moment, each of us is going through stages of an ever-changing, ever-evolving process."

The power of intention

> *You are what your deepest desire is.*
> *As your desire is, so is your intention.*
> *As your intention is, so is your will.*
> *As your will is, so is your deed.*
> *As your deed is, so is your destiny.*

—The Upanishads

The winds of grace are blowing—it is you who must raise your sails.

—Rabindranath Tagore

Deepak went on. "There is another important component that we don't talk about very much, because we don't really understand its implication and that is free will. We have the ability to choose. Rather than being led by chance and circumstance, we can exercise the power of intention, as expressed in this ancient Sanskrit poem from the Upanishads.

"And here is something that I wrote several years ago on this theme of intention:

Intention is the starting point of every spiritual path. It is the force that fulfills all of our needs, whether for money, relationships, spiritual awakening or love. Intention generates all the activities in the universe. Everything that we can see—and even the things we cannot, are an expression of intention's infinite organizing power.

As the ancient Indian sages observed thousands of years ago, our destiny is shaped by the deepest level of our intention and desire. Once we plant the seed of an intention in the fertile ground of pure potentiality, our soul's journey unfolds automatically, as naturally as a bulb becomes a tulip or an embryo becomes a child."[4]

"In other words, Jack, your intention is very much influenced by your intensity, your will, your vision, your capacity and your motivating influence. Let me try to explain it with an example: If it is your intention to climb Mt. Everest, you'll need tons and tons of motivation. But you'll also need tons and tons of capacity. Do you have what it takes, Jack? You'll need to practice every day for months and months to build up your endurance. Then you'll need to visualize, in your mind, over and over again, ascending the top of the mountain, in order to see every rock, obstacle, outcropping and crevice, committing it all to memory, so that you can, theoretically, scale the mountain with your eyes closed. After all that, you may be ready to tackle the mountain. You may not achieve your

---

[4] Deepak Chopra. *The Namaste e-Newsletter*, October 2008.

goal, but at least you will have the power of your intention. Do you understand?"

"Wow, I do understand. It took me a long time, but I realize now that as a created being I have the ability to make choices; free will is crucial to my maturation, as you have said so many times, and even though destiny has me on a path that gave me birth and unequivocally leads me to the end of life here, I can control the events in my life. That, coupled with intention lets me do whatever I want to do. And beyond that, love and empathy are necessary ingredients for living a good life. I now know what the recipe is. Deepak, do you want me to tell you what it is?"

"Of course, I'm listening."

"It's quite simple. Throughout the ages God has counselled us, and all His Messengers have repeated the same simple ground rule: the defining principle that resonates throughout all of man's history; Live your life by the Golden Rule.

In Zoroastrianism: Nature only is good when it shall not do to another whatever is not good for its own self. Whatever is disagreeable to yourself do not do unto others.

In Hinduism: This is the sum of all righteousness: Deal with others as you would yourself be dealt by. Do nothing to your neighbour that you would not have him do to you after.

In Buddhism: A clansman should treat his friends and familiars as he treats himself and should be as good as his word. Hurt not others in ways that you yourself would find hurtful.

In Judaism: Love your fellow as you love yourself. What is hateful to you, do not do to your neighbour.

In Christianity: Thou shalt love thy neighbour as thyself. Do to others what you would have them do to you, for this sums up the law and the Prophets.

In Islam: Wish for others what you wish for yourself. None of you is a believer until he desires for his brother what he desires for himself. Hurt no one so that no one may hurt you.

"The Golden Rule redefines all our humanity, our compassion for others and our common will to help one another. It is the only thing that will guarantee man's continued existence. I feel that I should tell you why that should be an epiphany at this particular moment. For I now realize that it is impossible to walk through a closed door into another room without trusting that we must acquire the knowledge necessary to enter what we call Heaven. The methods by which we acquire that knowledge are the belief in a Greater Entity and the applied disciplines of prayer and meditation. Consequently, we must apply our acquired knowledge for the good of mankind, as a testimony to the fact that we really understand the purpose for which we are put on this everlasting journey of existence."

Suddenly, I am confronted by a new figure, who greets me warmly, saying, "Hi, Jack, my name is Chief Tecumseh. I am a Shawnee chief. I could not help hearing your narrative with Deepak and his friends and I do believe that, as you have already said, the most worthy deed is service. I once wrote a poem about that that talks about man's mission in life:

So live your life that the fear of death can never enter your heart. Trouble no one about their religion; respect others in their view, and demand that they respect yours. Love your life, perfect your life, beautify all things in your life. Seek to make your life long and its purpose in the service of your people. Prepare a noble death song for the day when you go over the great divide.

Always give a word or a sign of salute when meeting or passing a friend, even a stranger, when in a lonely place. Show respect to all people and grovel to none.

When you arise in the morning give thanks for the food and for the joy of living. If you see no reason for giving thanks, the fault lies only in yourself. Abuse no one and no thing, for abuse turns the wise ones to fools and robs the spirit of its vision.

When it comes your time to die, be not like those whose hearts are filled with the fear of death, so that when their time comes they weep and pray for a little more time to live their lives over again in a different way. Sing your death song and die like a hero going home.[5]

"That's a wonderful poem. It epitomizes a life well lived. I think you got it."

THE END OF THE BEGINNING

---

[5] Chief Tecumseh, poem featured in the film *Act of Valor*.

REFERENCES

Aristotle. 2008. *Aristotle's Nicomachean Ethics.* Translated by Joe Sachs. Newburyport, MA: Focus.

Berger, P. L. and T. Luckmann. 1989. *The Social Construction of Reality: A Treatise in the Sociology of Knowledge.* Garden City, NY: Anchor Books.

Bisson, M. S., Nowell, A., Kordova, C. Kalchgruber, R. and al-Nahar, M. 2007. "Human evolution at the crossroads: An archaeological survey in Northwest Jordan." *Near Eastern Archaeology* 69, no. 2: 73–85.

Blackmore, S. 2005. *Consciousness, A Very Short Introduction.* New York, NY: Oxford University Press.

Bloom, A. 1968. *The Republic of Plato.* Chicago, IL: Basic Books.

Davies, P. 1992. *The Mind of God.* New York, NY: Simon & Schuster.

Egginton, W. 2001. *The Philosopher's Desire.* Redwood City, CA: Stanford University Press.

Ferguson, K. 1992. *Stephen Hawking: A Quest for a Theory of the Universe.* New York, NY: Bantam Books.

Fife, B. 1997. *The Detox Book.* New York , NY: Piccadilly Books.

Hawking, S. 1988. *A Brief History of Time*. New York, NY: Bantam Books.

Howe, M. 2001. *Genius Explained*. Cambridge, MA: Cambridge University Press.

Hughes, R. 1968. *Heaven and Hell in Western Art*. New York. NY: Stein and Day.

Jung, C. G, 2006. *The Undiscovered Self*. New York, NY: Penguin Books.

Krauss, L. M. 2012. *A Universe From Nothing*. New York. NY: Atria Paperback.

Momen, M. 1999. *The Phenomenon of Religion*. London: Oneworld.

The Office of Communications and Public Liaison National Institute of Neurological Disorders and Stroke National Institutes of Health. *The Brain* [NIH Publication No.02-3440d]. Bethesda, MD: Author.

Oz, M. and Roizen M. F. 2007. *You: Staying Young*. New York, NY: Simon & Shuster.

Plato. 360 BCE. *Timaeus*. Translated by Benjamin Jowett. http://classics.mit.edu/Plato/timaeus.html

Riordan, M., Tonelli, G. and Wu, S. L. 2013. "The Higgs at last." *Scientific American*, 12 August.

Schotter, A. 1981. *The Economic Theory of Social Institutions*. Cambridge, MA; Cambridge University Press.

Schultz, M. L. 1998. *Awakening Intuition*. New York, NY: Three Rivers Press.

Shiga, D. 2007. "The cosmos: Before the big bang." *New Scientist Magazine*, 28 April.

Tolle, E. 1997. *The Power of Now*. Novato, CA: Namaste Publishing and New World Library.

Wolf, F.A. and Toben, B. 1982. *Space-Time and Beyond*. New York NY: E. P. Dutton.

Made in the USA
Charleston, SC
03 June 2014